# FOREIGN TO FAMILIAR

## A GUIDE TO UNDERSTANDING HOT- AND COLD-CLIMATE CULTURES

English as a Second Language Edition

### BY

## SARAH A. LANIER

Foreign to Familiar (ESL Edition)
Copyright © 2021 by Sarah A. Lanier

The original English version of *Foreign to Familiar* was published in 2000 by McDougal Publishing, Copyright © 2000, 2020 by Sarah A. Lanier. ALL RIGHTS RESERVED

This ESL Edition has been published by:
McDougal Publishing
P.O. Box 3595
Hagerstown, MD 21742

ISBN 978-1-58158-200-0

Printed in the United States
For worldwide distribution

# REVIEWS

When I read the book, I recognized immediately that it has precisely the balance between adult-level concepts and clear language that I need in developing materials for intermediate and advanced ESL students. As someone who works cross-culturally, both on Guam and with the teachers I assist in the Asia Pacific Region, I am excited to find this comprehensible and respectful explanation of cultural differences. Please accept my compliments on an excellent job of intelligently simplifying and clearly explaining a complex topic.

— *M Johnson, ESL professor, Asia-Pacific Region*

I always recommend this book for everyone I know that goes abroad and everyone that reads it has the same response, "Now I understand why they do things so different in 'X' country." I've seen so many people's perspectives go from judging other cultures to understanding by reading this book. It's short, clear, easy to understand but so powerful. It is such an easy read you could probably finish it on your flight to wherever you are going. I live abroad and I make it required reading for anyone coming to visit.

—*A Fan*

This accessible, breezy, and clear primer summarizes both the author's intense personal experiences and significant amounts of "conventional sociological wisdom." College students, international aid workers, English teachers—along with international students, global trekkers, and world citizens—would benefit from investing an hour or two reading this fine, satisfying guide to understanding human beings born and raised thousands of miles from our hometowns.

-*Tony C., Professor*

# Acknowledgments

I want to acknowledge the extraordinary efforts of my friend Ricardo Rodriguez. He took many hours to explain to me how Latin leaders think and believed the effort was worth his time.

Michelle Wilson, who, as an ESL teacher with North Georgia Technical College, had the vision to turn *Foreign to Familiar* into a trainer for people studying English. She had been teaching her students about cultural understanding from the book by translating the English words as she read it to the class. She and her students went through every sentence to make them more accessible to those whose first language is not English. Without her, this edition would have never happened.

I want to acknowledge the countless friends who kept encouraging me to get my lectures into book form ... until I finally did. You know who you are.

# Contents

Preface ...................................................................................... 7

Introduction ............................................................................ 11

1. Differences Between Hot- and Cold-Climate Cultures ................ 14

2. Differences Between Relationship and Task Orientation ............ 22

3. Differences Between Direct and Indirect Communication .......... 30

4. Differences Between Individualism and Group Identity ............. 41

5. Differences Between Inclusion and Privacy ................................. 56

6. Different Concepts of Hospitality ................................................ 73

7. Differences Between High- and Low-Context Cultures .............. 82

8. Different Concepts of Time and Planning ................................. 110

9. Practical Next Steps.......................................................................... 124

10. In Conclusion ................................................................................. 133


Dictionary of Word and Phrases ...................................................... 135


Author Contact Page ........................................................................ 141

# Preface

The airplane was leaving on time. Three of us were buckled in, one next to the other, each finding it easy to make conversation. As the plane took off, we felt our problems from work leave us. We were off to *Glorietta, New Mexico,* for a week-long conference, and our minds were filled with thoughts of mountains and crisp air and a break from the Atlanta downtown routine. "So, Sarah," my aisle-seat **colleague**[1] said in that talkative manner of a tourist on vacation, "tell me what it was like growing up in the *Middle East*."

This was my least favorite way to begin a conversation. I had been hearing it ever since moving to the *United States* to begin my university studies. But, being in the middle seat, I could not escape.

I wanted to respond, "No, you first. Tell me what it was like growing up in a typical American home." What was there to

---
1. the people you work with; co-worker

say? And who cares anyway? But I did answer... "It was great," was my answer.

"No, I mean it, really," she asked again, "what is the **culture**[2] like over there?"

By the window sat Aida from *Lebanon*. She'd been in the *United States* eight years and was much more of an expert on *Middle Eastern* **culture** than I was. But, at the moment, Aida seemed to be very interested in what I was saying. So I decided to continue.

"Well, the Middle East has a variety of cultures. The European *Jews* and the *Arabs* are very different."

"How so?" she asked.

"In the *Jewish* **culture**, you say what you think. It is direct, and you know what people are thinking about you. I glanced at her to see if she was understanding me. She was, so I continued.

"The *Arab* **culture**, on the other hand, is much more indirect, never straight to the point. It's all about friendliness and politeness. If **offered**[3] a cup of coffee, I say 'No, thank you.'

2. the values and behaviors of a group of people
3. to give something that can be **accepted** or **rejected**

"The **host**[4] will **offer** it again, and I say: 'No, no, don't **bother**[5] yourself.' He might **offer** a third time, and I should reply, "No, I really don't want any coffee. Believe me.'

"Then my **host** will serve the coffee anyway, and I will drink it."

"You must be kidding!" she said, finding what I was saying hard to believe.

"No, really," I assured her. "You are **expected**[6] to **refuse**[7] the first few times. It's the polite thing to do."

"What if you really don't want the coffee?" she asked.

"Well, there are expressions you can use to say that you would not for any reason **refuse** their kind **hospitality**.[8] At some point in the future you will gladly join them in coffee, but right now you really can't drink it."

Now Aida got into the conversation. "This is amazing! I didn't know that!" she said, as our heads turned her way. "Aida," I replied, "what do you mean you didn't know that? You're *Lebanese*."

---
4. people who entertain guests (**host**, a man and **hostess**, a woman)
5. to annoy; disturb
6. being sure it will happen; **anticipated**
7. to say no; not take it
8. showing kindness to guests

"Yes," she said, "but I mean I didn't know this was not normal. I've been in the *United States* eight years already and did not realize it was done differently here. That explains so much.

"I have been lonely since moving here, and now I know why. When people in the office would ask me if I wanted to go to lunch, I would say 'no' to be polite, fully **expecting** them to ask me again. When they didn't ask me again and instead, left without me, I thought they didn't really want me to go with them and had asked only out of politeness. In my **culture**, it would have been too forward to say 'yes' the first time.

"This is why I have not had many *American* friends. After all these years, now I know why."

I sat there surprised and troubled. Thinking about the sadness of Aida's story, I said to myself, "No one should have to suffer like that simply because they don't understand the **culture** of another person." It is for the Aidas around the world I have written this book.

*Sarah A. Lanier*

# Introduction

The world is getting smaller as more people are traveling, immigrating, running from war zones and working **overseas**.[9] This change is creating **cross-cultural**[10] encounters at a faster rate. Modern media and the Internet add to **cultural** borders being removed. This makes us believe there are few cultural differences. In relating to one another, however, the truth soon becomes clear. It is easy for people to become **frustrated**[11] as **ethnic**[12] groups become divided and separated in opposing groups. Then people start to **defend**[13] their **cultural identities**.[14]

People are traveling **overseas** now more than any other time in history. Getting there is easy, but knowing how to

9. in a **foreign** country, especially one across a sea
10. **comparing** or dealing with two or more **cultures**
11. upset; irritated; annoyed
12. people grouped by race, nationality, **culture** or religion
13. be able to explain your reason for doing or believing something
14. who you are; the way you think about yourself

make friendships with the people they meet or live among is another matter. Even when people come home excited about the great response they had among the people of some other land, they rarely know the confusion they may have left behind them. Very few people who try to work with those of other **cultures** understand that the way they live out their **values**[15] and customs is probably completely **foreign**[16] to those they want to relate to. They can **expect** the **values** and customs of others to be completely strange to them as well. One book could never serve as a resource for all the **cultural** practices of the peoples of the earth, and this one does not try to do so. I have found, however, that there are **generalizations**[17] about groups of people that do help. **Cultural** differences can bring us great rewards and great pain. Simple conversations can create conflict. **Innocent**[18] comments can cause withdrawal and gossip. Living and working with people of different **cultures** used to be rare, but this is no longer

---

15. the worth, importance, or usefulness of something; **principles** considered most important
16. from another country; unknown; new
17. common ideas some people have about other people
18. not meant to cause harm

true. Everywhere we turn, we meet people with very different **values** and customs, and we often find them to be **offensive**.[19]

Most **cross-cultural** workers have few **cross-cultural** skills and, in some cases, do not even see the need to develop such skills. The sad thing is that he or she might mean to be kind but can be easily misunderstood, and this can hurt relationships with **colleagues** without the person even knowing it. I have written this little book of **cultural observations**[20] in response to repeated requests from those who have heard my **lectures**[21] on this subject. The book divides the world into two halves: "hot-climate" **cultures** and "cold-climate" **cultures**. It makes some **generalizations** that prove to be helpful if taken as that: **generalizations**. I trust that this book will be helpful to those who want to understand the differences between **cultures**.

---

19. causing someone to feel hurt or angry
20. to learn by watching carefully
21. an educational talk to students

# Chapter 1

# Differences Between Hot- and Cold-Climate Cultures

The **observation** that people of different **cultures** think, act and react differently is nothing new. Anyone who travels or knows someone from another country has **observed** this interesting fact. In my own country, the **observation** was made as early as the late 1700s by the *American* president, Thomas Jefferson. He noticed the difference between people living in different parts of the same country.

Like Jefferson's **observations** on *Americans*, the population of the entire world can generally be divided into two parts. The two groups are "hot-climate" (relationship-based: **focused**[1] on the relationship with a person)

---

1. **focus**, the center of interest or attention

**cultures** and "cold-climate" (**task-oriented**[2]) **cultures**. The idea of "hot- and cold-climate" **cultures** was first introduced to me by Ricardo Rodriguez, an *Argentine* lawyer living in *Chile*. When I went to live in *Chile* for nine months, I needed his help to make sense of the **culture**. I had grown up in the *Middle East*, lived eleven years in *Amsterdam, Holland*, and traveled all over *Europe*, the *Middle East* and *Africa*. I was from the *southern United States* originally and had returned there for university and postgraduate studies. Still, I was not fully prepared for the *Chilean* **culture** and did not understand its basic common characteristics.

Ricardo would spend hours with me talking about how the people thought, how the **Latin**[3] leader makes decisions and how the **culture** worked. In law school he had heard the term "hot- and cold-climate **cultures**," and he used it to help me understand what I was experiencing. What he said made sense to me: basically, that the *Latin* **cultures** are "hot," since relationship is the

---

2. the **focus,** focused on a goal
3. people from **Latin** America: the Caribbean; South and Central America

*Foreign to Familiar*

basis of everything, even in the work setting. **Northern Europeans**[4] seem more "cold climate," since the **focus** is on **efficiency**[5] and the task.

As I thought more and more about this subject, I began to see that the **culture** of the "**Southerners**"[6] in the *United States* had similarities to other "hot-climate" **cultures**, such as those of the **Latin Americans**. We were more like the *South Americans* than we were with our fellow *Americans* from the northern states. Similarly, the "cold-climate" *Israelis* of *European* background had more in common culturally with the **Dutch**[7] than with their fellow "hot-climate" *Jews* of *Middle Eastern* background.

Some countries, of course, did not follow that pattern as easily. *Russia*, for instance, has cold weather most of the year. Being mainly **agricultural**,[8] however, *Russians* act more like "hot-climate" people. When I examined this more closely, I found this true of most rural or tribal societies.

---

4. people from Germany, the Netherlands, Switzerland and Scandinavia
5. doing things well
6. people from the Southeast in USA
7. the people of the Netherlands
8. farming; raising crops/animals

## Differences Between Hot- and Cold-Climate Cultures

Among these are **indigenous**[9] *Alaskans*, the mountain village people of the *Andes*, the *Himalayas* and other such areas, and the *Eastern Europeans*.

As I have spoken to people from many different **cultural** backgrounds, I have found that identifying **cultures** in these two categories, "hot and cold" climates, has provided simple ideas that help us understand how some **cultures** are alike. This has brought healing, prevented conflict, and helped in planning and problem solving among groups that work **cross-culturally**. The most rewarding result of this project has been to see people come to understand others who are different from themselves. With this understanding they can **accept**,[10] rather than **avoid**[11] those relationships.

After I gave a **lecture** on this subject in *India*, a group of *Nepali* men from *Nepal* came to me. Two had tears in their eyes. The spokesman for the group said, "We want to know why we were never told before how *Europeans* think. Although they are our **colleagues**, we have been hurt by them for years. For example, when they asked us to take

9. the **native** people of a country
10. to receive
11. to keep away from or stop yourself from doing something

*Foreign to Familiar*

them on **treks**[12] into the *Himalayas*, we would, of course, say yes, as our **culture** requires. How were we to know that they did not understand our **culture**? We really meant 'no,' but were unable to say 'no' directly because they were guests in our country.

"We did not know they didn't understand our **culture**, nor that we were really saying 'no.' We would have to leave our families without food or money, often for a month at a time, causing great suffering to us and to them. If we had only known these **concepts**[13] about the differences in the way we and the *Europeans* think and communicate, we would not have experienced pain and broken relationships."

A similar conversation took place in *Geneva, Switzerland* ("cold-climate") after I had spoken to a group of professional women. The director of a division of the United Nations in *East Africa* ("hot-climate") came to me. Obviously quite emotional, she said, "I'm an *African*. I have worked among *Scandinavians* (people from *Denmark, Norway* and *Sweden*)

---
12. a long difficult hike, often many days or weeks
13. ideas

## DIFFERENCES BETWEEN HOT- AND COLD-CLIMATE CULTURES

for fourteen years here in *Switzerland*. If I had only known what you are teaching when I first came, I would have understood my **colleagues'** behavior was not **rudeness**,[14] or **rejection**,[15] but just **cultural** difference. To this day, I have very few friendships among them, because I did not understand the basics of their **culture**."

Why would the climate make such a difference in people's **culture**? There are many **theories**[16] about this. It may be the difference between farming-and factory-based economies. It may have to do with the cold weather keeping people indoors more. If they are more to themselves, they are less dependent upon their neighbors. Perhaps in the hot **cultures** people live more connected to the land and, with it, more dependence between neighbors. This would make relationships more important.

I have a **theory** that the whole world was at one time much more "hot-climate" and that only with the **Industrial**

---

14. disrespectful; not polite
15. not being **accepted** or liked
16. possible reasons for ideas

*Foreign to Familiar*

**Revolution**[17] and the use of more structured time did that change come in certain societies. Whatever the case, it happened, and we must **accept** it if we are to get along with our neighbors.

Among the "cold-climate" regions, I would list *Canada*, the *Northern United States*, *Northern Europe* (*Switzerland* and above), *Israel* (the ***Jewish*** population that came mainly from *Europe*), the white populations of *New Zealand*, *Australia*, and *southern Brazil* and the white population of *South Africa* and any other countries or parts of countries largely settled by *Europeans*, such as *Argentina*.

Among the "hot-climate" **cultures**, I would include the *Southern United States*, *Asia*, the *Pacific Islands*, *South America* (an **exception**[18] would be much of urban *Argentina*, which is eighty percent *European*), *Africa*, the *Mediterranean* countries (**except** the ***Jewish*** population of *Israel*), the *Middle East* and most of the rest of the world.

Wanda, a farmer's daughter from *South Georgia* ("hot-climate") in the *United States*, said, "I spent twelve years in

---

17. (1760-1840) A time when Europe and the USA developed factories
18. something that does not follow the rule or is not included

## DIFFERENCES BETWEEN HOT- AND COLD-CLIMATE CULTURES

the *Philippines* ("hot-climate"). From the time I got off the plane, I was at home there. The **Filipinos**[19] were friendly, **unstructured**,[20] **inclusive**[21] and **laid-back**,[22] like we were back home in *Georgia*. Other people talked about **culture shock**.[23] I wondered what their problem was."

Why was a "hot-climate" *Georgian* able to find so much in common with "hot-climate" *Filipinos*? Some clues lay ahead ... .

Read more to find out.

---

19. people from the Philippines
20. doesn't follow a schedule
21. everyone is welcomed and included
22. relaxed and calm
23. the impact of getting use to a different **culture**

# Chapter 2

# Differences Between Relationship and Task Orientation

The story is told that President Jimmy Carter upset the **Western**[24] news people when he met with *Egypt's* Anwar Sadat and *Israel's* Menachem Begin for peace talks. As the media waited and waited to report the news, the leaders sat behind closed doors drinking coffee. One day passed, then two, with the only news being that of angry reporters wanting to know why no news of their progress was being shared. Meanwhile, inside, the three men were getting to know the names of each other's grandchildren, relationships were being made, and trust was being built. After three days,

---
24. people from the West part of the world; Western Europe, North America

## Differences Between Relationship and Task Orientation

a new relationship was built, and the **Camp David Accords**[25] were the result.

Jimmy Carter was a peanut farmer from *South Georgia* and a "hot-climate" man. He knows all about taking the time necessary to build trust. After his presidency, he has carried the honor and respect of being one of the most effective **mediators**[26] with "hot-climate" leaders around the world.

One of the most important differences between the "hot- and cold-climate" **cultures** in the work setting is that the "hot-climate" **culture** is relationship-based, while the "cold-climate" is task **oriented**. Coming originally from **the** *South*, I understand the **concept** of relationship-based **culture**. In **the** *South*, conversations between people are friendly and often **superficial**.[27] Everybody there knows this. When going into a store, it is the custom to speak first, to be friendly. You might mention the weather, something in the news, or something else to start a conversation. Even the simple greeting, "Hi, how are you?" will do in many cases.

---

25. an agreement between Israel and Egypt in 1978 that led to a peace treaty
26. a person that helps others in conflict come to an agreement
27. fake; on the surface

*Foreign to Familiar*

Once this "feel-good" atmosphere is established, you may then ask what you need, without being too **curt**.[28] It would be **acceptable** to say something like, "Could you help me with something? I'm looking for the hardware section." It would not be **acceptable** to say something like, "I need some nails." That would not be considered friendly.

If I say to someone in **the *South***, "I just got my hair cut. What do you think of it?" even if my hair looked terrible, the response would always be. "It's REAL NAAS." Translated, this means "It's real nice." Truth is not the **focus** here; keeping a friendliness between us is.

What is the reason for this reaction? All "hot-climate" communication has one goal: to promote a "feel-good" atmosphere, a friendly environment. Truth is secondary to the relationship. No one is willing to risk the friendliness, no matter if it is **superficial**, to tell the truth about my hair. Let me find out how bad it looks some other way.

I told this to a close friend who happened to be a **Southerner**. She laughed about the hair example and said that although she saw it was true in **the *South***, she

---
28. replying with a very short answer, almost **rude**

## Differences Between Relationship and Task Orientation

**preferred**[29] to tell it like it is. Only a few weeks later, I came home with a terrible haircut. It was way too short. The same friend insisted she liked it. Then, as I was driving off, she called after me, "And don't worry. Your hair will grow back." This proved that she really didn't believe my haircut looked good.

In "cold-climate" *Holland*, on the other hand, **accurate**[30] communication is **valued**. If I asked a friend in *Holland* what he or she thought of my haircut, the **focus** on the most **accurate** answer to my question would be with no thought of how that answer might affect my feelings. The answer might be, "It makes your face look fat." If I said, "Well, that hurts my feelings," the person would answer, "What do feelings have to do with it? You asked my **opinion**[31] about your hair. This isn't about you; it's about your hair."

In "cold-climate" **cultures**, personal feelings are kept separate from **objective**[32] issues. A short, seemingly **curt** answer is often mistaken by the people of "hot-climate"

---
29. what a person likes
30. correct in all details; exact
31. belief; judgment; viewpoint
32. an **opinion** outside of yourself; removed from your feelings

*Foreign to Familiar*

**cultures** as being **rude**. They might even feel **rejected**. They take the **curtness** personally. In fact, the "cold-climate" person may be very friendly and warm, but when needing to get a job done or answer a question factually, he or she is completely focused on the task that needs to get done. Rightly or wrongly, personal feelings are not a part of the situation.

If we were talking about personality differences rather than **culture**, we would call "hot-climate" types 'feeling personalities' and "cold-climate" types 'thinking personalities.' These are terms used by Isabel Briggs-Myers to describe a difference in personalities in regard to how people make decisions—on their **subjective**[33] feelings or on their **objective logic**.[34][35]

The "feeling"-type person usually has people as the primary **focus** and combines the task and the relationship so as to be "relational" while getting the job done — even if it means the job gets delayed at times to attend to the relationship. The "thinking"-type person has the task or

---
33. an **opinion** influenced by personal feelings or tastes
34. a decision based on reasoning, not feeling
35. *Gifts Differing* by Isabel Briggs-Myers, Consulting Psychological Press.

### Differences Between Relationship and Task Orientation

goal as **priority**[36] and separates the task from the relationship — even if it means neglecting a person's feelings to get the job done.

Those who have this **priority** do not mean anything personal by putting the job first. They **assume**[37] you think the same way. "Feeling" types also **assume** that you think like they do, and that's why they are **offended** by your attitude and actions.

We all have our personality **preferences**, regardless of our **cultures,** but our **cultures** also have personalities. Even if we are high on relationship or "feeling" and we live in *Minnesota*, a "cold-climate" state in the *United States*, we learn to be short and **to-the-point**[38] in a business transaction. We learn to respect the other person's time and to try to be as quick and **efficient** as possible out of respect for the person and the task.

Even if we are "thinking" types in our personalities, if we live in a "hot climate," a feeling-**oriented culture**, we learn that it is **acceptable** to greet with a smile and be friendly. **Efficiency** is not usually as important as making sure the

---
36. the most important part
37. to believe something without proof
38. said without wasting words or time

*Foreign to Familiar*

person feels welcomed and cared for. When we understand each other, we can make the necessary **adjustments**.[39]

In the "hot-climate" world, words are often used as a means of establishing a pleasant atmosphere. This means the **literal**[40] meaning of the words is not as important as important as making a connection with the person.

This is clear in the experience of a friend of mine who was traveling in the *Middle East* ("hot-climate") on Yemeni Airlines. A flight attendant came by and said, "Excuse me, sir. Would you like coffee or tea?"

"Oh, I'd love to have a cup of coffee, please," he replied.

To this, she answered, "I'm sorry, we only have tea."

For the "cold-climate" person who **expects** words to be **accurate** and mean what they say, her answer was strange and confusing. To the Yemeni flight attendant, her words were only meant to be polite.

---

39. changes
40. exactly as it is written

## POINTS TO REMEMBER

**"Hot-Climate" Cultures:**
- Are relationship based.
- Communication must create a "feel-good" atmosphere.
- Though the individuals may be otherwise, the society is feeling **oriented**.
- **Efficiency** and time do not take **priority** over the person.
- It is inappropriate to "talk business" upon first arriving at a business meeting or making a business phone call.

**"Cold-Climate" Cultures:**
- Are task **oriented**.
- Communication must provide **accurate** information.
- Though individuals may be otherwise, the society is **logic oriented**.
- **Efficiency** and time are high priorities, and taking them seriously is a statement of respect for the other person.

## Chapter 3

# Differences Between Direct and Indirect Communication

Another important difference between the "hot- and cold-climate" **cultures** is in the way people communicate. Most people communicate in an indirect or direct way. In "hot-climate" **cultures** that **emphasize**[41] relationship, being indirect is a way to **avoid offending** the other person and keeping that "feel-good" atmosphere. It is also a way of making sure that one's own **preference** is not forced upon another person. The "cold-climate" person, because he **values** being **accurate**, will be direct. He will answer the question as **efficiently** as possible. Here are some examples:

---
41. give special importance

## Differences Between Direct and Indirect Communication

A person is driving to town and a friend asks if he or she can ride along. The driver, if indirect, will say something like, "I'd love to give you a ride, but I'm not sure how much space we will have yet. The car holds five, and six people have already asked. Maybe we can fit you in." He is probably sure he doesn't have enough space, but he doesn't want to say this.

In **contrast**,[42] in the "cold-climate" **cultures**, saying exactly what you think is a way of respecting the other person's need for **accurate** information. "I'm sorry, but we're full." That is not **rejection**; it is information.

Once, when I was teaching on the subject of **culture** in a course in Hawaii, my students were from many different countries. When I talked about the indirect, relationship-based means of communication in most "hot-climate" **cultures**, a *German* ("cold-climate") man in the class spoke up. "I can't imagine this is true. Why would people not just say what they think when you ask them a question?"

A *Filipino* ("hot-climate") responded, "But it *is* true. That describes my **culture**."

---
42. differences can be seen

*Foreign to Familiar*

The *Germa*n, in his direct way, said, "Well, I think that is **ridiculous**."[43]

A little later, I had the class break into groups of four for **discussion**.[44] There was an *Asian* ("hot-climate") couple in the class. Because the wife's understanding of English was not strong enough to understand the **lecture**, her husband translated for her. This kept her from participating in the class **discussion**. But then I noticed that she was speaking up during the small group **discussion**.

When everyone had come back together, I thought this might be a great opportunity for the class to hear from the *Asian* lady, and I asked her if she would report back for her group. "You can feel free to speak in your language," I encouraged her, "and your husband could translate for you, if that's okay."

She smiled and nodded, "Be happy to. Be happy to."

An *American* in the class spoke up and said, "Sarah, didn't you do that wrong? You asked her a direct question, and she is going to say 'yes,' even if she means 'no' because

---
43. absurd; silly; foolish; unbelievable
44. talk about something; share ideas

## Differences Between Direct and Indirect Communication

she can't tell you 'no' directly. At least, that's what you just taught us." Realizing my mistake I said. "You are absolutely right. I did it wrong." I turned to the husband and said, "Would you ask your wife if she would mind speaking for her group."

He asked her in their language, then he turned back to me and said, "She asked that she please not be required to share in class. It would be very embarrassing for her. She begs not to be required to do so."

The *German* sat there surprised. He could not believe what had just happened.

Here's another case: "Where is the nearest post office located?" **Frustrated** tourists in *Turkey* or the *Philippines* or some other "hot-climate" **culture** have asked this question many times and received a very friendly response and even directions. But, when they followed the directions, they were disappointed to discover that the post office was not where they had been sent. Why did this happen? Sometimes a village doesn't even have a post office. Sometimes a person is trying to be helpful and does not want to disappoint the person asking the question with bad news. So, he or she

*Foreign to Familiar*

gives a friendly answer, just to create a friendly atmosphere. The answer may or may not or be **accurate** at all.

So how do you get to the truth? Direct questions should be **avoided**. Why? So that the person being questioned is not **shamed**[45] for not having the correct answer. To find out about the location of the post office, therefore, you may need an indirect way to ask.

One method would be to ask a man on the street if he would ask the man on the corner if he knows where the post office is located. In this way, the man on the corner can be free to say to the messenger, "No, sir, I don't know where it is." He is free to say this because he is not disappointing a visitor to his country. He is just responding to the messenger. In many countries you will discover that the direct way of asking often doesn't result in the answer you are looking for.

If you have a "hot-climate" roommate, and you want to know if your music is **bothering** him, it is useless to ask directly, "Is my music **bothering** you?" The answer will usually be, "No, it's fine." If you really want to know, you must be indirect.

---
45. public humiliation; embarrassing; making someone look bad in public

### Differences Between Direct and Indirect Communication

This can be done in a **variety** of ways. You might ask, "What is your favorite kind of music?" If the music is off, you might ask, "When do you like listening to music?" Again, the best method would be using a third person. Say to the person, "Could you ask Mario what he thinks of my music?" For people of "cold-climate" **culture**, this seems a dishonest way to find out your information, but in the "hot-climate" countries, this is very **acceptable**. It is a way of learning the truth without causing someone to be hurt, angry or upset. And that is of the greatest importance.

The people of "cold-climate" **cultures** find this **roundabout way**[46] of doing things to be crazy. "Why can't they just say what they mean? Why can't their 'yes' be a 'yes' and their 'no' be a 'no'?" they ask. The answer is that the goal of the speaker is friendliness. This isn't about the information; it's about friendliness.

If you were to say 'yes' the first time to the coffee, you would appear too forward, too eager, and the coffee would become the **focus**, not the entertainment of guests.

As I said before, if you enter a hardware store in *Georgia,* another "hot-climate" **culture**, and say directly, "Five pounds

46. indirect, not clear

*Foreign to Familiar*

of nails, please," you would be considered **rude**. You are **expected** to say something pleasant and **superficial** before stating your business, like "How's it going? or "You doing all right today?"

If you were to go into a *Dutch* hardware store talking that same way, the owner would become **frustrated** because it would be seen as wasting his time. There, you can just politely say, "Hello, I'd like five kilos of nails, please." There is no reason to ask how the person is feeling that day. That's none of your business. It's personal information and is kept for family and close friends.

Buying the nails and making the purchase is the important thing. Short answers, in this case, are not **rude** but are part of being **efficient** and professional.

After living in *Holland* I developed a "cold-climate" approach to communication. So when I moved to *Chile*, I would often forget to use the indirect approach. I'd finally agreed with some of my **Latino** friends that we had two languages: "directo" and "indirecto."

I asked Gladys one day if she would go to another town in *Chile* with me.

## Differences Between Direct and Indirect Communication

"O, si, si, quiero ir contigo," (yes, yes, I'd like to go with you,) she answered.

Then I remembered to make sure, and I asked her, "¿Hablas 'directo' o 'indirecto'?" (Are you speaking direct or indirect?)

She smiled and admitted, "'Indirecto,' es verdad. No quiero." (Indirect, it's true. I don't want to go.)

In a rural town in northern *Argentina*, I had shared these **concepts** with a group of friends. My **hostess**, who, up until that point had been warm and friendly, suddenly changed. She started saying 'no' to everything I asked. She disagreed with me in small ways every time we spoke. After a few days, I became worried. What had I done to make her so against me?

Finally, I went to her and asked what I had done to **offend** her. She answered, "Oh, Sarah, you haven't done anything to **offend** me. You said I need to learn to say 'no,' and so I'm practicing." Saying 'no' directly was so **foreign** to her that she could not do it gracefully.

When I returned to **the *South*** of the *United States* a few years later, these lessons were helpful. It takes skill and

*Foreign to Familiar*

understanding dealing with the situation to find out what a "hot-climate" person truly wants! A simple 'yes' or 'no' is rarely the answer to a question.

## POINTS TO REMEMBER

### Direct Communication: ("Cold-Climate")
- Short, direct questions show respect for the person's time, as well as professionalism.
- A 'yes' is a 'yes,' and a 'no' is a 'no.' There are no hidden meanings.
- An honest, direct answer is information only. It does not **reflect** on how the person feels about you.
- You can say what you think (nicely), and it will usually not be taken personally.

### Indirect Communication: ("Hot-Climate")
- It's all about being friendly.
- Every question must be phrased in such a way as to not **offend** by its directness.
- Use a third party for **accurate** information if you sense that a direct question will be too harsh, or not get the results you are seeking.
- A 'yes' may not be an answer to your question. It may be the first step in beginning a friendly interchange,

or verbal compliance may be required by the **culture**. Therefore, **avoid** yes-or-no questions.
- **Avoid** embarrassing people.

## Chapter 4

# Differences Between Individualism and Group Identity

In his book, *Cultures and Organizations*, Geert Hofstede, a **Dutch** psychologist, gives us another serious **cultural** difference to consider: the individual and the collective in society.[47] I will refer to the collective as "the group." The "group" **concept** is found in most "hot-climate" **cultures.** The **concept** of the individual or "individualists" are found more commonly in "cold-climate" **cultures.**

In most "cold-climate" societies, from the time children are small, they are taught, "You are an individual. Learn

---
47. Chapter 3, "I, We and They," with Gert Jan Hofstede and Michael Mindov, New York, NY, McGraw Hill: 1991

*Foreign to Familiar*

to think for yourself." Children from these countries know that they should have an **opinion** and be able to **defend** that **opinion**. An individual who thinks for themselves and is independent are considered to be very good qualities. In the *United States*, one of the **founding**[48] **values** of the country is that the individual has certain rights. "I have my rights" is something you will hear an American say when he doesn't feel he is being treated fairly. Another part of that "individualism" can be: "I will look out for myself, and you look out for yourself."

In most "hot-climate" **cultures** (the *Southern United States* is one of the **exceptions**), the opposite is true. Children are taught, "You belong. You belong to a family, to a tribe, to a village. (The *Maoris* of *New Zealand* have a saying, "I belong; therefore I am.") Your actions **reflect**[49] on the whole group. You must behave in a way that brings honor, not **shame**, to the family name. We all take care of each other. No one stands alone."

There is a "group" belief that says, "We are a community and must share our food, private lives, homes and even

---
48. what something was built on
49. to represent the whole group, to speak for the group

## Differences Between Individualism and Group Identity

**opinions**. This is done to serve the whole group." This thinking translates into a behavior that includes others and is not independent, no one is left out.

A common mistake that I have seen made in international **gatherings**[50] is to ask all the people there to give an **opinion** on a certain subject. An *American* (individual) will gladly stand up and give his or her **opinion**, but the *Kenyan* (group) will not. He will not speak until he has time to **discuss** it with the other members of his group. If he already knows how the group feels about a certain subject, he can speak. But when he speaks he is not representing his own **opinion**. He is representing the general **opinion** of the group. The result is that "one" *Kenyan* (group) voice may represent "twenty" other people individuals, while one *American* (individual) voice may represent just that one person. The leaders of international **gatherings** may need to find ways to give more importance to the **opinion** shared by a person representing his "group" **culture**.

For example, in a conference where twenty languages were represented, the principal language was English.

---
50. when people meet together

*Foreign to Familiar*

All the meetings were in English, and so were most of the workshops. The leaders of the meetings were mostly *Europeans* and *Americans*. They were **discussing** whether or not to have translation from the **podium**[51] or to have separate translations for the **various** language groups to save time. As **various** individuals voiced their **opinions**, it was clear that the separate translation for each group was the **preference**.

Then a man from *Bolivia* (group) spoke up and quietly explained the difficulty translators have with this type of translation. They are only able to hear half sentences because they don't have time to finish translating a sentence before the speaker is moving on to the next thought, speaking at the same time. He also explained that speaking one language at a time during translation helps those who speak English as a second language. The pause for the translator, after each sentence, slowed the speaker down so all could understand. This also allows the other translators time to hear full sentences and translate them before the speaker continues.

---
51. the place the speaker stands so all in the audience can see and hear him

## DIFFERENCES BETWEEN INDIVIDUALISM AND GROUP IDENTITY

The head of the leadership heard the *Bolivian* (group), but then said, "Good point, but the **majority**[52] seem to think it is not worth the loss of time to speak one language at a time." What he failed to recognize was that the *Bolivian* (group) man was representing the **majority**. The others who **preferred** this method were not speaking up, because they had been represented and did not need to be heard as individuals.

The people of the "individualistic" **cultures** all spoke up for themselves, so they seemed to be the **majority**. Add to this the fact that the "hot-climate" people were "indirect" in their communication and, so, less likely to speak their **preferences** "directly." The result was that we had a poor representation of the desires of the **majority** of the people.

"Individual" **identity contrasts** with "group" **identity** in other ways. One afternoon, as I was walking in my neighborhood in *Amsterdam* (individual), some teenage *Arab* (group) boys started following me. They were making **rude** remarks in Arabic with someone who was unaware of what they were saying. To their surprise, I understood.

---
52. the greater number

*Foreign to Familiar*

I turned around and boldly asked them. "What is your family name?"

Shocked that I understood what they were saying, they asked, "Why do you want to know?"

I said, "I want to know which families you boys belong to, so I can tell your fathers how you are behaving in public. When your fathers hear how you are **shaming** the family by your behavior, they will give you the discipline you need."

"No! No!" they begged. "Please don't tell our parents. We were just joking around and didn't mean any disrespect. We're sorry." And they quickly ran away.

I had guessed right. Because they were from an *Arab* (group) **culture**, their group **identity** was strong. This meant that the actions of each individual **reflected** on the family, the village and even the tribe. In "group" **cultures**, the individual does not stand alone and is never the only one affected by his own actions. The mention of their families made the boys realize that they could not get by with bad behavior without it affecting their families.

### Differences Between Individualism and Group Identity

## When "Individualists" Visit Poor Societies In Group-Oriented Cultures

In the *United States*, the economy has been strong since overcoming **the Great Depression**.[53] Food has not been hard for most people to find. So, the way people in the *United States* view food has changed. At one time, people ate to **nourish**[54] their bodies; they ate to **survive**.[55] Now eating has become something to be enjoyed and a form of entertainment.

**Variety** and flavor in foods are important to *Americans*. They enjoy making choices when it comes to eating. When *Americans* travel to a country where the main role of food is still a source of **nourishment**, they may not realize how **offensive** it is if they **refuse** food that is given to them just because they might not like it. "Liking" food is not important in those countries. In a poor country or in a poor family almost anywhere, the **priority** with food is filling the stomach, not having a **variety** of foods or a special taste in foods.

---
53. (1929-1939) A time of worldwide financial **crisis** which started in the USA
54. to give what is needed for health
55. being able to continue to live even when it is very difficult

*Foreign to Familiar*

Once, while we were preparing a team of *American* young people to go to a poor country, one young man asked me, "But what do we do if we don't like the food?"

I said, "You eat it. It's about relationship with your **hosts**. Eating the food is an **acceptance** of their way of treating guests, and this has a higher **value** than the taste of the food."

The "individualist" usually decides what he or she likes or dislikes. In "group-**oriented**" **cultures**, this is not a **priority**. In many cases, the people do not even ask themselves the question, "Do I like how this food tastes?" They just eat what they have, enjoying it because it is filling them up or because it is being generously **offered** to them.

Ricardo, my advisor, once said, "Sarah, in the countries where there has been wealth for several generations, there is an **orientation** toward **comfort**[56] and **convenience**.[57] These countries, however, are relatively few. In most countries of the world, the **orientation** is toward **justice**[58] and **survival**. Having what is necessary is important. Having extra is only for celebrations or some special occasion."

---

56. the feeling of being relaxed and happy
57. is easy and not much work
58. concern for fairness; equality and respect for all people

## Differences Between Individualism and Group Identity

When a **host** family that is poor puts out a large amount of food for their guests, they may be cooking up several days' worth of food to show their **generosity**.[59] They will then feed their own family with whatever food is left over. Some guests feel that they need to eat everything, but the truth is that leaving some behind might be very much **appreciated**.[60] It's worth checking out the local customs before visiting a home in an unfamiliar **culture**.

Enjoying **comfort** and expensive things is more common to places like the *United States*. **The Great Depression** is only a memory for the older generations, and no major war has affected the economy as bad in the past one hundred years. For this reason, people from wealthy nations (or wealthy families in any nation) who are guests of the poor should be careful not to waste food or other limited resources. Unnecessary waste can be painful for some people to see. They think only of how hard they have worked to get the food they have **offered** you.

---

59. being kind and giving
60. to be very important to a person; **valued**

*Foreign to Familiar*

## Individualism Versus Group Orientation In A Team Context

For the "individualist," being a team member generally means being an **equal**[61] to the other team members. A leader has a **role**[62] to fulfill, but probably does not **expect** to make all the decisions. So, especially among **Westerners**, the team members, as "individualists," often speak up to their leader or **take initiative**[63] in the group based on their knowledge of the subject.

This is not usually true with "group" **cultures**. In those **cultures**, the **role** of the leader is stronger, often more as a director. The group members often wait to be asked rather than risk **asserting themselves.**[64]

What is sometimes called "the Tall Poppy Syndrome" may also be something to consider. This term refers to the fact that if one member of the group **takes the initiative to assert** himself. They "lop" off the tall poppy to be on

---
61. having the same social status; no one is superior to the others
62. a job or position of the person
63. to speak up, make suggestions or step forward
64. putting themselves in charge; taking control of a situation

## Differences Between Individualism and Group Identity

the same level with the rest. In *East Africa*, I was told, "If a nail sticks its head above the rest, we hammer it down."

People of "individualistic" backgrounds may not understand this and will **expect** to see personal initiative, or at least honest feedback from each team member. If the person from a "group" **culture** has not been given a **role** to support **taking that initiative**, he or she may find it extremely **foreign** to do so. To the group, **roles** are important, as they provide order for their society. It is equally confusing when a person from an" individualistic" **culture takes initiative** in a team when it is not his or her **role** to do so. If this **initiative** is seen as unacceptable to the person's position, he or she may be **ignored**[65] or even severely corrected.

A team of young people from "individualistic" **cultures** went to *Africa* for three months of service. The team leader was *African*. Some of the team members later complained that they were not included in decisions or communicated with personally on what was happening. They were just "told what to do." As I talked with the leader later, he was

---
65. to intentionally not give any attention to someone

*Foreign to Familiar*

surprised to hear that they felt a need for communication. From his **perspective**,[66] he had told them what they needed to know when they needed to know it.

In "group" **cultures**, it is **expected** that the leader will lead, and the team will basically follow. (This can change with the type of team or group involved, especially within the individual customs of a country.) Team members, out of respect for the leadership, are **expected** to cooperate and not pull against the authority of the leader. This may be a challenge to some who feel they are giving up their **identity** to do so. To think in terms of "we" instead of "I" can be a major change in thinking for some people from "individualistic" **cultures**.

The opposite will be true for a person who has left his "group" **culture** to visit or study in an "individualistic" **culture**. The **loneliness**[67] of being left to oneself can be **overwhelming**[68] at first. Also, the challenge of making decisions based on what the individual wants or **taking initiative** based on the individual's ideas alone may seem **rude** to them.

---

66. personal viewpoint
67. feeling alone, not included in the group
68. very great amount; more than someone can handle

## DIFFERENCES BETWEEN INDIVIDUALISM AND GROUP IDENTITY

A *Filipino* ("hot-climate") and a **Dutch** student ("cold-climate") are sharing a **dorm**[69] room with three others. The *Dutchman* is playing very loud music. He says to his *Filipino* roommate, "Does my music **bother** you?"

It's the wrong question. A person who is not **oriented** toward speaking out loud his own **preference** would look around to the others to see if the other members of the group mind the music. Also, being from a "hot-climate," the *Filipino* cannot say directly what he thinks, if it in any way causes a problem for another. So, he naturally responds, "No, no, it's fine."

"Are you sure?" the *Dutchman* asks.

"Yes, of course. It's fine," he is assured. The truth is that the *Filipino* cannot stand the music. At the same time, his response has not been a lie. Besides the fact that his **culture** will not allow him to say so openly, he does not even mind dealing with an **inconvenience**[70] for the sake of the group. It is a normal thing for him to do. The important thing, to him, is the peace of the group and

---
69. a place students live at a school
70. something that is un**comfortable** and difficult

*Foreign to Familiar*

what the group wants. He was not raised to consider his own **comfort** first.

The *Dutchman,* raised as an "individualist," was taught to look out for himself and to let his **preferences** be known when anyone asks.

## POINTS TO REMEMBER

### Individualistic Culture ("Cold-Climate"):
- I am a self-standing person with my own **identity**.
- Every individual should have an **opinion** and can speak for him- or herself.
- **Taking initiative** within a group is good and **expected**.
- One must know how to make his or her own decisions.
- My behavior **reflects** on me, not on the group.

### Group-Oriented Culture ("Hot-Climate"):
- I belong, therefore I am.
- My **identity** is connected to the group (family, tribe, etc.).
- The group protects and provides for me.
- **Taking initiative** within a group or not can be determined by my **role**.
- I do not **expect** to have to stand alone.
- My behavior **reflects** on the whole group.
- Team members **expect** direction from the leader.

Note: The *Southern United States* is a "hot-climate" **culture** that does not necessarily fit into the group orientation.

## Chapter 5

# Differences Between Inclusion and Privacy

One of the "group" **identities** common in the "hot-climate" **cultures** is what we call "inclusion." Inclusion means that people are automatically included in everything happening in their **presence**.[71] This would include a conversation, a meal, a television program, a sport being played or most anything else. It also means that when two people are having a conversation, it is not thought to be a private conversation. Therefore, a friend may feel free to walk up and join them.

In "individualistic" **cultures**, privacy is very important. This means that people have a right to privacy, whether

---
71. where they are right now

## Differences Between Inclusion and Privacy

in a conversation, a meal or a quiet space to themselves. Therefore, an approaching friend must understand the other's need for privacy and start any "**intrusion**[72]" with a question or an **apology**.[73] Phrases such as "Am I **interrupting**[74]?" or "Do you have a minute?" or "Is this a good time to ask you a question?" showing respect for the other people.

Most "hot-climate" **cultures** are **inclusive**. In *Chile* or *Egypt* or other "hot-climate" **cultures**, I know that I can join in with whatever is going on in my **presence**. This includes plans being made and food being shared.

My sister visited me once while I was living in *Chile*. She's a lot of fun, and my friends loved being with her. The only trouble was that I had to translate for her, since she didn't speak Spanish. My Spanish had improved just enough that I could translate for her on a **casual**[75] level.

As we walked through town with these friends, my sister was excited to talk about everything she saw. These comments were directed at me, but because I knew it

---
72. an uninvited visit or entrance
73. to say "I'm sorry"
74. to stop the activity
75. **comfortable** and relaxed

*Foreign to Familiar*

was **rude** for the two of us to carry on a private conversation in the **presence** of my friends, I translated all of her comments and questions to the others. They enjoyed her remarks and smiled because they were being included in the conversation.

After hours of this, I was very tired and asked that my sister comment less. It was just too tiring to translate it all. She was able to stop for a while, but it was hard for her to keep quiet about all the new things she was seeing and experiencing. She's a person who likes to express her excitement in words.

I finally turned to my friends and asked, "Is it okay if I don't translate everything my sister says? It is just too exhausting. If it's all right with you, I'll just let you know when she says something important?" They all laughed and said they understood. We agreed this was best for all of us.

With the "hot-climate" people, there is little difference between who is a part of an event and who is not, at least on a social level. It is **rude** to mention going to the movies in the **presence** of someone you don't plan to **invite**.[76] In fact, in

---
76. when you are asked to go somewhere or do something

## Differences Between Inclusion and Privacy

many parts of the world, any person who overhears your plans **assumes** "inclusion" and would be surprised to learn they're not included. In these parts of the world, privacy is not understood. It seems like people are left out. It is seen as **rude**.

I was **invited** to the home of a friend for dinner in *Chile*. It had been over a year since we had seen each other, and our plan was to catch up on the news of friends and share photos. I was hoping for an evening of private conversation with just the two of us.

While we were still eating, a knock came at the door. The door opened, and a man came in. He pulled up a chair and joined us. We forgot our conversation and talked with this man about local news.

Then another knock on the door brought another visitor. This visitor also joined us. With the arrival of this new visitor, the subject of our conversation was once again changed. The two visitors stayed until midnight, and we enjoyed the visitors very much. Our own plans for the evening were forgotten.

What seemed strange for me was the fact that my friend thought nothing of this **intrusion**. He had lived in *Chile* long

*Foreign to Familiar*

enough that he no longer considered our visit to be a private one. It had become, for him, an "all-**inclusive**" event.

The **"inclusive" cultures** also see food as something to be shared. The people in these places would never take out a sandwich in front of others and not **offer** to share it. I am told that there is a saying in Japanese, "Even if you only have a single pea, you divide it up equally with the number of people in the room." In these **"inclusive" cultures**, there is no **concept** of "Will there be enough for everyone?"

The *Maoris* of *New Zealand* (**inclusive**) also have a proverb: "You bring your basket, I'll bring mine, and together we'll feed everyone." The important thing is that the food is shared.

I was traveling on a bus in *Thailand* (**inclusive**) with other speakers returning from a meeting. I had packed a lunch for the four-hour ride. Having learned about "hot-climate" inclusion, I brought fruit, cookies and other items that could be shared. About lunchtime, two *European* (private) men in front of me took out their packed lunches and began to eat. That got me hungry, so I got out my lunch too.

## DIFFERENCES BETWEEN INCLUSION AND PRIVACY

I **offered** the men some grapes. They said, "Thank you, but we brought our own lunches." They also **refused** the cookies. Then I got up and **offered** the grapes to others around me on the bus—*Africans*, **South Americans** and *Asians*. They all happily **accepted** the food and then pulled out their own food to share. Soon we were handing around bags of dried figs, potato chips, bread, cheese and other items. We had a feast that day.

The two *Europeans* enjoyed their own lunches, but they missed the more important event. It wasn't as much about food as it was about sharing with one another, leaving no one out. By including those who had nothing to share, the group took care of them. And, because everyone shared, we were not aware of those who had something to share and those who did not. They were covered by the community. The "inclusion" **value** of "hot-climate" **cultures** means that no one is left out, and no one is **lonely**.

When I lived in *Amsterdam* (private), a common topic of **discussion** among **colleagues** was the **loneliness** of the city. I spent years trying to come up with a solution with others what to do about our feelings of **loneliness** and **lack**[77] of relationships.

---
77. not enough

*Foreign to Familiar*

Then I lived in *Chile* for nine months. At the end of that time, I realized I had never met a **lonely** person. It was almost impossible to be **lonely** there. People were always **dropping in**,[78] sitting in your kitchen while you cooked, and talking with you. If you wanted to be with people, you just walked out your door and started visiting. If you did not want to be with people, you had to hide.

My sister loves people and does very well in the "inclusion" **culture**. She once said, "I could never get tired of people. Just pile them on. Leave me a little room to breathe, but pile the people on." While visiting me in *Santiago, Chile* she felt sick one evening and went to lie down in our bedroom. A friend came by to see me and sat on my bed to talk. Soon, the room was full, as usual, and some were sitting on my sister's bed. No one seemed to notice that she was trying to rest. But this did not **bother** her. She loved it.

As a "cold-climate" person, my greatest **sacrifice**[79] was giving up my privacy, my time to myself. I never knew

---
78. to visit someone unannounced and **unexpected**
79. giving up something that is very important to you

## Differences Between Inclusion and Privacy

when I might be **interrupted**. This seemed exhausting until I got used to it. Then it became normal to me.

Soon after returning to *Amsterdam* from *Chile*, one Sunday afternoon I cooked up some food, which I often do just for the fun of it. I then called around to friends to **invite** them over that evening to eat. I was disappointed that no one could come. I would get the response: "I would ordinarily have loved to come, but I was planning to just relax tonight," or "Oh, if I had only known earlier. I have taken a bath and do not want to go back out. How about if we do lunch on Tuesday?" Well, that was nice, but I wasn't **lonely** at lunchtime on Tuesday. I was **lonely** on Sunday night. Still, because of the need my friends had to plan everything out ahead of time, I wasn't able to convince a single one of them to come over. That's when I realized a reason for the **loneliness** in our well-organized city. What we needed was some "hot-climate" unplanned relationship and a little less "cold-climate" structured privacy.

When I returned to the *United States*, I missed being with **Latinos**. In fact, I was **lonely** in general. One night I went to the local all-night restaurant for a cup of coffee, just to

*Foreign to Familiar*

be around people. From where I was sitting, suddenly I heard Spanish being spoken. I was now aware of the "inclusion" **principle**[80] of "hot-climate" people and **assumed** most Spanish-speaking people would be from some "hot climate."

I greeted the Spanish speakers in their language. I told them I had just returned from *Chile* and missed hearing Spanish being spoken. Just as I **expected**, the mother moved over in her seat and waved me over to join them. I brought my cup of coffee from the other table and settled down **comfortably** at their table like an old family member.

They were a *Mexican* family on vacation in the *United States*. The father was a doctor and had looked forward to this trip for years. He told me, however, that I was the first *American* to extend a welcome to them. They had been surprised at how private everyone seemed to be. They were not complaining; they were just thrilled to have an *American* relate to them the way they would relate to a visitor in their country.

In many "hot-climate" **cultures**, **gatherings** outside the workplace are family **gatherings**, and children are part of

---
80. rule, idea

## DIFFERENCES BETWEEN INCLUSION AND PRIVACY

the picture—noise and all. This may be **frustrating** for those from the individualistic and privacy-**oriented cultures**, as they feel the **distraction**[81] of children running in and out takes away from the **quality**[82] of the event.

I once attended a meeting in *South America* where the mothers wanted to be involved in some major decisions being made. Naturally, they brought their children with them, since the **concept** of getting a babysitter was **foreign** to most of them. At one point, the noise and commotion got so bad that the adults were spending most of their time keeping the children in line. Because it was such an important meeting to these people, I **offered** to take the children (all fourteen of them) to my house for a video.

Later, when the parents came by to retrieve their children, they thanked me profusely and expressed their amazement at how much they were able to accomplish without all the **distractions**. To my "cold-climate" **values**, the task of the meeting was unquestionably the

---
81. something that takes your attention away
82. how good something is

*Foreign to Familiar*

**priority**. To my **Latino** friends, being together with the whole family had become the higher **value**—even with a business meeting. I was in their country, so eventually I learned to tune out the children and focus on the **discussions** at hand.

When traveling in privacy ("cold-climate") **cultures**, a common mistake made by those from **inclusive cultures** is to **assume** that their children are included in **invitations**. They have very little experience with "**adults-only**"[83] events and need to realize that in cases such as weddings, when children are **invited**, they are **expected** to stay with their parents. And, if they make noise, they should be removed.

When visiting privacy **cultures**, people from "hot-climate" countries should make a point of clarifying whether or not an **invitation** includes children. It is better to find out ahead of time who is included. To show up with four children at someone's home for dinner and then discover plates set only for the adults leads to unnecessary hurt feelings.

---

83. any activity to which children are not **invited**

### Differences Between Inclusion and Privacy

### Shared Possessions

In the individualistic **cultures**, **possessions**[84] are treated as the personal responsibility of the individual. He is the **steward**[85] of them, must take care of them, and has the right to share them or not share them. From a young age, a child is taught to take care of his bicycle, his toys and his other **possessions**.

In the inclusion **culture**, this is reversed. Most everything is "ours," not "mine." A member of the family will say, "We have a guitar." "We have food in the refrigerator." This "we" will include everyone in the house, not just those who live there. "We have tools to use"—regardless of who paid for them.

A student just arriving in *Hawaii* from *China* came to his **dorm** room after his *American* roommates had already left their luggage and gone out. When they returned, they found their suitcases opened. Their clothes were out, and the *Chinese* student was trying them on. The two *North American*

---
84. what you own, what belongs to you
85. owner, manager

*Foreign to Familiar*

students went into a rage at this invasion of their privacy, leaving the *Chinese* young man confused and **shamed**. His introduction to America was one of wounding. He was from a **culture** where (particularly with the influence of Communism) everything was shared. He had no **concept** of how individualistically *Americans* viewed their things.

In the worldview of the *Chinese* student, it was not "I have shampoo," it was "We have shampoo." It was not "You have a suitcase full of clothes, and so do I," but "There are clothes here to be worn. Let's see which ones fit me best."

In many countries with **inclusive cultures**, I never go anywhere alone. Whether it is driving or walking, someone else comes along to keep me company. If I would **insist**[86] on driving to the store alone, this would probably be seen as a **rejection** of others.

In the same way, if a car is going to town and there is space available, I know I can ask to go along. I witnessed a man seeking a ride from an *American* couple on their way to town. They turned him down, wanting time to themselves. Their decision was based on a need for privacy. The man

---
86. to demand; not allow someone to say no

felt **rejected**. To the **inclusive** person, it is never "I am going into town," it is "We have a ride to town."

Some excerpts from my personal journal illustrate this conflict:

*Yemen, September 14, 1999:*
*I have had a hard time trying to find time to work on this book. I had to look at my itinerary to see where I might grab some "alone time." I have found it [time] here in Yemen. This is an inclusion **culture**, but I'm with **Westerners** who have heavy workloads themselves, and they totally **appreciate** my need for time alone. So, my housing is very private, and when I'm not in meetings it's okay for me to stay by myself to get writing done. I go from here to East Africa and will be almost exclusively with Africans, who would probably feel badly for me if I had to be alone.*

*Uganda, October 1999:*
*I am in lovely Uganda. I was shown my room. It was simply furnished with a bed and a mosquito net. Next to*

*my bed another mattress had been placed on the floor and a makeshift mosquito net tied to the window to cover it. My **hostess** said, "Here is your room, but don't worry. I have put a person in here with you, so you won't have to be alone."*

I smiled and thanked her for her thoughtfulness.

## POINTS TO REMEMBER

**"Hot-Climate" (Inclusion) Cultures:**
- Are group **oriented**.
- Individuals know they are automatically included in conversation, meals and the other activities of the group.
- **Possessions** are to be used freely by all: food, tools, etc.
- It is not desirable to be left to oneself.
- It is **rude** to hold a private conversation or make plans that prevent others from participating.

**"Cold-Climate" (Privacy) Cultures:**
- People enjoy having time and space to themselves.
- People are **expected** to ask permission to borrow something or to **interrupt** a conversation.
- Each person is considered to be the **steward** of his or her **possessions** and has the responsibility to maintain and protect them.

- In a community setting, it might be common to put a label on your food, tools, etc. to set them apart from the group's common **possessions**.
- It is **acceptable** to hold private conversations or make exclusive plans with a few people, not including everyone.

## Chapter 6

# Different Concepts of Hospitality

In the "hot-climate" **cultures**, generous and friendly treatment of visitors and guests is the **context**[87] for relationship. It is a way of saying, "I am **offering** a relationship out of which we can do business." This is not the same as a personal relationship, but it is a relationship. **Hospitality** involves food and/or drink and is usually done in the home.[88]

In the *United States*, it is more common to take someone out to a restaurant to do business or even to entertain a

---
87. the setting or surroundings
88. An **exception** to this may be China, where the people entertain guests in restaurants more often than **inviting** visitors into their homes. This might be due to the modesty of their homes or also because Chinese food takes a long time to prepare, and so it's easier for the Chinese to entertain in a restaurant.

*Foreign to Familiar*

visitor. This would not be considered good treatment of visitors in the "hot-climate" **cultures**. It is not personal enough. To bring someone into your home is to say, "I **offer** to relate to you personally."

On a **casual** day-to-day basis, entertaining guests and visitors may be something as simple as **offering** a cup of tea or **insisting** that you stay to eat with the family. It is not thought of as being a **formal**[89] occasion that requires a special menu or the need to clean the house first. Being ready to do something without having planned it first is a part of entertaining guests and visitors. This can mean meeting the need for a meal when it is suddenly needed.

When I first went to *Chile*, I was looking forward to how the people treated guests and visitors and **assumed** that I would be **invited** into their homes. But the first month I was there, nothing happened. I was saddened by this. I enjoyed doing things with the people during the day, but I wanted very much to be a greater part of their lives.

---

89. the opposite of **casual**; very polite and official, involving special customs and clothing

## Different Concepts of Hospitality

Finally, one day I shared how I was feeling disappointed with Ricardo, the man who gave me advice. He laughed and said, "Sarah, they are hurt that you haven't come by. You stay to yourself at night like you don't want to be with anyone else. We don't send out **invitations** around here. You just come by."

"But how can I 'come by' when I don't even know these people?" I asked.

"That's just the way it's done," he said. "Only '**formal**' occasions, those requiring special clothes, need an **invitation**. The rest is unplanned."

"But what if people are busy or want to be left alone? How would I know when to come over?" I asked.

"Sarah," he told me, "you just don't understand. Your coming over will never **interrupt** them. They will continue cooking, playing with the children or watering the garden. You will just fit into whatever is going on at the moment. They will not stop what they are doing to sit in a **formal** living room with you."

"If you are concerned that people may want to be alone." he told me, "in our **culture**, people come first, and our own

75

*Foreign to Familiar*

desires come last. We would never give up an opportunity to **host** guests for some time alone."

I learned that he was right. Soon I was visiting people, and they loved it.

## Hospitality and Traveling

Because **hosting** guests in the "hot-climate" world is mostly done without planning, they do not think "We weren't planning for you, so you need to find a hotel." If a person shows up **unexpectedly**,[90] that person is fully aware that he or she was not **expected**, so it isn't a problem. A place on the floor would be fine for most of those who know you are unprepared for their arrival. The important thing for them is to be able to stay with people they know or can trust.

In most "hot-climate" **cultures**, treatment of visitors means taking in and caring for those who are traveling. If you are visiting someone's home, they take full responsibility for your needs. They give you a place to sleep in the house, they feed you and entertain you. You are not

---
90. you did not know it would happen

## Different Concepts of Hospitality

**expected** to pay for anything. You are staying in their home, and this means they will provide all your needs. However, it *is* **expected** for the traveler to **offer** a gift to the **host**.

When a "hot-climate" person travels to the *United States* or *Northern Europe*, they often don't know just what to expect. Being "individualistic," the people in "cold-climate" **cultures** believe the traveler is responsible for his own needs. If housing is **offered**, that is special treatment of guests, but they **assume** that the person traveling has his own travel plans and even his own means for eating out.

One of the surprises a **foreigner** meets the moment he arrives in some "cold-climate" countries is that he needs money to **survive**. He even needs money to rent a cart to remove his luggage from the airport. (Most of the world's airports provide such carts free of charge or have men to carry the bags, and **offering** a tip to them is left to the decision of the traveler, but not in many *European* and *North American* airports.

Many travelers from "hot-climate" countries, if they have very little money, have saved, **sacrificed** and received gifts from family and friends to purchase their airplane tickets. Once they are on the airplane, they **assume** that they will

*Foreign to Familiar*

now be guests. When their food is provided on the plane, this makes them feel that they will be cared for by their **hosts**. They do not realize that many American families have never even thought this was their responsibility.

If a **foreign** guest is part of a trip to the beach, his friends may suggest going to get ice cream and **assume** he has money to pay for his own. (This is more common in the *United States* than in *Europe*.) This surprises the visitor, for he is unaware that **hosts** are responsible only for what they have agreed to in advance. The **shame** he feels when standing there with the ice cream seeing his friends walking off with theirs is very painful. He may not have enough money with him to pay.

In most "hot-climate" countries, in fact, in most other countries of the world outside of the *United States*, if someone says to you, "Let's get a hamburger," it means "I'm **inviting** you to go, and I will pay." I rarely find a visitor to the United States who has not learned this custom the painful, **shameful** way. Usually they have finished the meal by the time they learn that they are paying for their own meal, and they either don't have the money with them, or they wish they had known ahead of time so that they could have made other plans. They were really not interested in eating out and went only because they thought they were responding to an **offer** of relationship.

Those who are preparing to go to the *United States*, therefore, must plan to take along some spending money. This will save them many hurt feelings. It they don't have money with them, it can be difficult for them to talk about it with their **hosts**. It might be kind for a **host** to include a small envelope of money in a welcome basket for a guest if he knows that guest has little cash with him.

These are simple lessons, but they help us to understand each other as people travel more and more.

# POINTS TO REMEMBER

"Hot-Climate":
- **Hospitality** is **spontaneous**[91] (unplanned), often without any advance **invitation**.
- **Hospitality** is the **context** for relationship (even a business relationship).
- **Hospitality** usually takes place in the home.
- The **host** fully takes care of the needs of the guest. The guest pays for nothing.
- A gift is usually **expected** from the guest.
- Food and drink are involved.
- Travelers stay with the **host** and every need of theirs is taken care of.

"Cold-Climate":
- **Hospitality** is taken very seriously and is planned for.
- **Hospitality** is usually not as **spontaneous**. The **host** usually needs to know ahead of time before a visit takes place.

---
91. unplanned

- Travelers are **expected** to plan to stay in a hotel, unless it has been planned and agreed upon with the **host** ahead of time.
- Guests need to **expect** to pay for their transportation and restaurants if visiting the *United States*. If the **host** plans to pay, he will usually say so.
- **Hospitality** is a special occasion, taking the full attention of the **host**.

## Chapter 7

# Differences Between High- and Low-Context Cultures

There is another category of culture that cannot be **ignored**. It has to do with whether a culture is "**formal**" (arranged in a very orderly and regular way) or "informal" (not arranged in a very orderly and regular way). Edward T. Hall, in his book *Beyond Culture*,[92] speaks about **formal culture** as "high-**context**" and to informal **culture** as "low-**context**." A "high-**context**," or **formal culture** is one that has been around a long time. *Switzerland*, for example, is more than eight hundred years old, and the **Swiss**[93] have had time to build tradition upon tradition, collecting many rules that everyone seems to know except the **foreigner**.

92. New York, NY, Anchor Books: 1976
93. people from Switzerland

## Differences Between High- and Low-Context Cultures

In the smaller villages, traditions remain stronger than the cities. Everything matters in small towns in *Switzerland*. It matters how high you grow your bushes. It matters when you put your trash out on the street. It matters that you bring a gift when you visit someone's home. It matters how you dress when you go shopping downtown on a Saturday morning. In the towns of *Switzerland*, it is easy to recognize a tourist. Middle-aged women, if they are wearing tennis shoes downtown, will not be **Swiss** women. A woman from *Switzerland* would be dressed up and wearing her high heels to go shopping.

In a "high-**context**" **culture**, everything matters. There are rules for everything. This includes how you eat, how you greet others (especially the way young people speak to older people), wedding traditions, table manners, who you know, etc. The "high-**context**" community has a rule for every situation. Everything matters.

Another thing that is different in "high-**context**" **cultures** is that they have not mixed with other **cultures** very much. Villages are usually "higher-**context**" than cities because cities usually have people from many different **cultures** that

*Foreign to Familiar*

have moved in over time. In the *United States*, in *New York*, an *Italian* family may have its traditions which the children grow up knowing are important. Outside the home, however, in the school and on the streets, these customs and rules may move over for the mixture of other **cultures** that make up the neighborhood.

If it is a custom for the people of *Yemen* ("high-**context**") to require their teenage girls to keep their heads covered. That rule is supported by the local community. But, if a *Yemeni* family moves to *New York*, their children will go to school with *Irish, Italian* and *African-American* young people who do not cover their heads. So daughters will soon be asking their parents if they can wear the head covering only when other *Yemenis* are around and leave it off when they go out. They want to fit in to the mixed **culture** of the city. Some "high-**context**" immigrants stay together in large cities, creating **ethnic** neighborhoods, where they can keep their "high-**context**" customs and traditions.

Cities that have stayed the same and have not been influenced from outside **cultures**, are more "high-**context**." *Damascus,*

## Differences Between High- and Low-Context Cultures

*Syria,* is an example of that kind of city. "Low-**context**" **cultures** are young or mixes of **cultures**. *Australia* and the *United States* are both less than two hundred and fifty years old and continue to add new **ethnic** groups. There has not been a **monocultural**[94] people living in these countries long enough to develop a "high **context**" among the people living there.

The **indigenous** people—the *Aborigines* of *Australia*, the **Native**[95] *American Indians* and the *Maoris* of *New Zealand*—are "high-**context**." They have been there for hundreds of years as one **culture** and have not changed as much. Therefore, their traditions and rules are extremely important to them.

The *Southern-California* **culture** is an example of "low-**context**," or informal, **culture**. It is a young society, with people moving in and staying there only since the late 1800s. In *California*, anything goes, and nothing matters. It doesn't matter what you wear to religious services. There are few social rules that people are **expected** to follow.

In fact, those who live in *California* feel a sense of freedom to be creative, start new **trends**[96] and be different. This **lack**

---
94. single **culture**
95. a person born in that place
96. to do what others are doing; a fad

*Foreign to Familiar*

of **context** has even made it possible for some who would be **rejected** at home to make a new start there. **Interracial**[97] marriages, for instance, are **rejected** in most" high-**context**" towns, but are common and **accepted** in *Southern California*.

**Native** *Californians* ("low-**context**") often do not understand why such things as "**proper**[98]" wedding rules of behavior mean so much to a family from the *Northeastern United States* ("high-**context**") or in the older, more "high-**context**" states. In fact, **Native** Americans and Mexican families who have been in California for more than three hundred years, are typically more "high-**context**." There are always new people coming to *California*, making it a mixture of many **cultures**, so there is not one main **culture** leading the others. There is an informality in the language, dress and manners of the *Californian* that makes him look very different when he is **overseas** or in a "high-**context**" **culture** such as *Switzerland* or an *African* village.

The *Jewish* nation of *Israel* is another young **culture**, just over seventy years old. The general population is

---

97. people from different races or **ethnic** group coming together
98. right; correct; **accepted**

## Differences Between High- and Low-Context Cultures

completely **casual**. Government officials in Israel often wear open-necked shirts or even shorts to the office. The military is also more **casual** than most, with officers and subordinates often **addressing**[99] each other on a **first-name basis**.[100] The reason for all of this is that, when *Israel* became a nation in 1948, *Jewish* people from all over the world moved to *Israel*, making it so there was no one main **culture** in *Israel*. Of course, there are small pockets of "high-**context**" **culture** in *Israel*, as there are in all countries where **ethnic** groups choose to live together. These would include the *Yemenite*, *German* and *Orthodox Jewish* communities, among others. Each of these has its own strict traditions and rules.

The *Arab* communities in *Israel* are more "high-**context**." They see their traditions, rules and ways of **addressing elders**[101] or superiors by their **title**[102] as a matter of honor and respect. If you go to an *Arab* home for a meal, there are rules to follow. For instance, dressing up is **expected** as a way of honoring your **host**. Bringing a gift, having very

---
99. how you greet someone
100. using your **given name** in an informal friendly way
101. a person who is older
102. a name that tells a person's position; doctor, teacher, Mr., Mrs.

*Foreign to Familiar*

polite conversation and knowing when to leave are other ways to show respect.

In some cases, there are **signals**[103] you should be aware of. For instance, the serving of the coffee may **signal** that the visit is ending. In this case, you would not want to leave until the coffee is served. It's important to find out ahead of time what the **expected** and **accepted** rules of behavior are. This is changing now in the younger, more globally connected places. The Internet has exposed most "high-**context**" **cultures** to new or different **trends**.

Can you imagine peace in the *Middle East* ever happening without the **various** people there first understanding the great differences between each other's **culture**?

*Korea* is five thousand years old. Now that's an old **culture**! Imagine the many traditions and rules that have had time to build up there. From the time a *Korean* child is born, he is constantly being instructed on what is **acceptable** and what is required in his **culture**. Authority goes with age and position. The older a person is and the higher position they

---

103. an action or sound that is used to communicate information or instructions

## Differences Between High- and Low-Context Cultures

have give them more respect and authority. **Titles**—such as Teacher, Mr., Mrs. and Officer—go together with each person's name, and the **given name**[104] is never used without the **title**. Obeying these rules of behavior is **expected** at all times.

Until very recently, a *Korean* going **overseas** usually considered his **customs** to be normal. When he meets the informal ways of the *Western World*, he is often surprised and thinks of this as a **lack** of respect for himself and others. One *Korean* friend came to work on an international team in a "low-**context**" **culture** and was very surprised to find that everyone was on a **first-name basis**. Even the children called adults by their first names. Staff members called their supervisors (on all levels) by their **given names**. My *Korean* friend was not **comfortable** with this. He felt that it was dishonoring and tried to use "Mr." for himself and others. It didn't work, and he finally gave up.

At first, the rest of the staff went along with his request. But, later, when he asked that he be greeted and recognized when anyone entered a room he was in, this was too much for some of those from other nationalities. They

---
104. first name; the name given to you at birth; the name people call you

*Foreign to Familiar*

did not take the time to **discuss** their own traditions and **cultural** rules. Instead, they argued with him and became angry. The two groups became **divided**.[105]

Another *Korean* friend of mine came to work in that same country. She knew that it would be difficult and painful for the first few years. Soon, however, she learned to change hats (**roles**). She wore her **Western** hat where that was **acceptable** and switched back to her *Korean* hat when around *Koreans*. Another good thing that came from her ability to change was that she became a **culture bridge**[106] for other *Korean*s who traveled outside of their nation. She didn't become a **Westerner**, but she was definitely a person who knew how to relate to **Westerners**.

It is important to mention that since the 1990s the **culture** of *Korea* has been quickly changing with international travel, the Internet, technology, news media, etc. The *Korean* young person is becoming more **westernized**.[107] Many say they are a new kind of *Korean*. Still, they know the **values** of the earlier generations and, for the most part, are very respectful toward them.

---
105. split into parts; separated
106. a person who can help others understand new **cultures**
107. to become like the people who live in the **Western World**

### Differences Between High- and Low-Context Cultures

## Who You Know

In "**context**" **cultures**, *who* you know is more important than *what* you know. Who you are related to matters. I learned this the hard way back in my grandparents' hometown in the southern *United States*. I moved there after knowing the town only through visits to my grandparents. I knew **Southerners** were friendly people, so I was **expecting** to be welcomed **with open arms**.[108] I was amazed when I went into a store and asked to open a credit account there, but the owner would not let me open the account.

Because I grew up **overseas**, I no longer had the **Southern accent**[109] of my childhood. This owner thought that I was a "Floridian." Because of the growing crime rate in Florida's cities, people there were buying land in our area and moving to Georgia. Now all **outsiders**[110] moving into the area were called "Floridians." It didn't matter if they were from *New York* or *China*, they were still a "Floridian."

---
108. eagerly, warmly, wanting to please; happily
109. a way of pronouncing words
110. a person who is not a part of the group

*Foreign to Familiar*

A week or two later I decided to go back in and try opening that account again. When I told the man my plans, he said, "Well, okay. Give me your address so we'll know where to come for deliveries."

I said, "Do you know where Homer Cook's property is?"

He said, "Well, sure."

I said, "He was my granddaddy, and I live on the back side of his property."

"You're Homer and Annette Cook's granddaughter?" he said. "Why, there's no finer folk in the county than your grandparents. Your granddaddy fixed an old dresser that belonged to my grandparents, and then he gave it back to us after my grandparents died. It's the only thing of theirs I have. He was a fine man."

His attitude had now totally changed. "Sarah," he said, "it will be a pleasure doing business with you." I had not changed, but I was now "in context," and suddenly I was **accepted**.

This is also true for those moving into "high-**context**" locations where they have no connections with others. In

## Differences Between High- and Low-Context Cultures

some cases, those who don't have a connection can remain "**outsiders**" for many years. Some may want very much to be **accepted** by the **locals**.[111] They go out and introduce themselves or try to have conversations with people they meet in churches or places of business. They may find that people will be friendly at first, but often the friendship will not be very deep. The **locals** don't yet know how these new people will fit into their **context**.

Being introduced by people who are very respected in the community can make all the difference. When they approve of you, that gives permission for others to approve of you also, even though you are a new in the community.

I have *European* friends who did this right. They moved to a *Middle Eastern* city (a "high-**context**" community) to learn Arabic and needed housing. They knocked on the door of a family in the city, asking if they had a room available. The family did have a room they were willing to rent to them. My friends later learned that this was one of the oldest and most respected families in the city. This family had lived there for eight hundred years, and many respected

---
111. a person from that location; a **native**-born person

*Foreign to Familiar*

city leaders had come from this family. My friends became respected in the community by knowing this family. Just by being in this family's household, they carried the family name, and doors of relationship were opened to them. Within a few short weeks of being in the country, they were more **accepted** by the *Arab* society than other **foreigners** who had been there for years. The secret was being in the **proper context**.

## How You Dress

In "high-**context**" **cultures**, because everything matters, that includes how you dress. Even in poor areas of the world, the people dress their very best when going to a meeting, out in public or to someone's home for dinner.

For a "low-**context**" person, wearing **comfortable** shoes and **casual** clothes when traveling may seem fine, but that would be considered **rude** by the **host** in a "high-**context**" culture. Dressing **casually** says, "I don't respect you or your rules, and I show this by not

## Differences Between High- and Low-Context Cultures

dressing in an **acceptable** way."

Modern *Australians* and *Americans* can be **guilty**[112] of this. They may feel being **comfortable** is more important than looking **acceptable**. There has been a slow change in the way *Americans* think and feel since the 1960s. I still remember my grandmother, living in a small "high-**context**" town, getting dressed up because she was going to town. Grandmother's trip to the post office and bank meant putting on a nice dress, lipstick, a hat and dressy shoes and carrying a nice purse. If I started out of the house in my play clothes to go with her, or I was dirty or too **casual**, she would send me back inside to wash up, put on a nice outfit and comb my hair. Being **properly** dressed mattered.

I still remember when flying on an airplane was a dress-up occasion. Men wore coats and ties. Women dressed in their finest clothes. **Comfort** was not the consideration.

When flying internationally these days, travelers are commonly seen wearing a **variety** of clothing, from dark,

---
112. doing something wrong

*Foreign to Familiar*

**formal** suits to **casual** sportswear. My guess is that the dressed-up people are from "high-**context**" **cultures** or subcultures, as a business.

Today, few *American* tourists get on an airplane without **comfortable** clothing and tennis shoes, unless traveling on business. Their **casual** appearance stands out in **contrast** to the suits and ties and dresses and matching shoes of the international travelers on the same plane.

Many young people also dress **casually**. In most **cultures** they make up the "low-**context**" side of the **culture**. They may be testing their family's rules, expressing their individuality or copying celebrities of other **cultures**. Young people are often more open to change, **accepting** new ideas or new people, simply because they want to know what is outside their **context**.

When going into "high-**context**" societies, the rule is to look around and see how other people are dressed. It is better to be **formal**, so as to show honor, rather than to dishonor your **host** or the people you hope to relate to. When in doubt, dress up.

### Differences Between High- and Low-Context Cultures

## "Power Distance"

Many "high-**context**" societies are known to have a greater "power-distance" than the more **casual** "low-**context**" **cultures**. Dr. Geert Hofstede came up with the phrase *"Power Distance,"* in his book, *Cultures and Organizations, Software for the Mind.*[113] The phrase means there is a great social distance between the levels of authority. For example, the relationship between a teacher and student, officer and soldier, boss and employee, even parent and child is more **formal**. Usually, the more **formal** the society the greater the distance between those in authority and those under them. **Addressing** authority with **titles** and showing **proper** respect is **expected**.

This is common in most of the world, but the young societies (such as previously-mentioned *California* or *Israel*) have a lower "power distance." Children might call their teachers by their first (**given**) names and get by with talking without respect to their **elders**, and employees might question their bosses openly. This would not happen in countries where

---
113. With Gert Jan Hofstede and Michael Mindov, New York, NY, McGraw Hill: 1991

*Foreign to Familiar*

the "power distance" is greater, such as *South Africa* or the *Asian* countries. Respect for an **elder** or someone of superior status is **expected** in "high-**context**" **cultures**.

The **casual** friendliness that may be common between university professors and their students in *California* would not happen in *China*. Younger *Koreans* are telling me this is true mostly with the older *Korean* generations, but, the *Korean* youth also know how to show respect to their **elders**.

The **casual** *American* or *Australian* can **offend** a *Korean* by **addressing** him or her by the first name. This informality is seen as disrespect.

While communicating in the work setting, an *Australian* team member may feel the freedom to challenge the supervisor or team leader on an idea, simply because, for him, the "power distance" is not great. He **assumes** he has the freedom to give his **opinion**, as one whose **opinion** is **equal** in **value**. But a team member from a "high-**context**" **culture** may be upset by what seems to be a **lack** of respect.

My *American* (low-**context**) cousin lived in *Thailand* (high-**context**) for a year. While helping a young man with

## Differences Between High- and Low-Context Cultures

his English lessons, she discovered that his teacher had made some mistakes in grammar. My cousin wanted to bring these mistakes to the attention of the teacher, but the **Thai**[114] student was horrified that she would even consider correcting a person of authority.

When teaching a **multicultural**[115] class in *India*, I **offered** a class one evening. The class was **optional**[116] for those who wanted to attend. There were 150 students in the daytime class, and 25 of those students were *Korean* (high-**context**). I was surprised when all 25 of the *Korean* students showed up to the evening class. Some were obviously tired, yet they came. Later, I realized that they had come only because I had **invited** them. They could not disappoint their teacher by not coming.

To **avoid** this mistake, when I **offered** an **optional** class the next night, I said, "It is my request that you not attend my class if you need time with your family or if you need the time to work. If this is not a subject that you have a great need for, may I encourage you to take the time to work on your other

---
114. a person from Thailand
115. several distinct **culture**s
116. can choose to do it but you don't have to

*Foreign to Familiar*

schoolwork. You would dishonor me if you came unnecessarily." This surprised them. They laughed, knowing what I was doing. That night, only five of the *Koreans* showed up for my class.

This was one of the reasons for the indirect communication that was necessary in *Hawaii* with the *Asian* woman I mentioned in Chapter 3, Direct Versus Indirect Communication, pages 31-34. Not only was the woman's communication style "indirect," but I was the **lecturer** and, therefore, the person in authority she felt she needed to obey. I was thinking she would simply tell me if she wanted to speak or not, based on my "lower-**context**," low-"power-distance" **cultural** background.

## Gender Differences

In the **cultures** where there is great "power distance," there are also **gender** differences, differences between men and women. I learned that, as a *Western* ("low-**context**") woman, I should not try to force my "freedoms" on the women of other **cultures**. More importantly, I learned not to be **offended** when men of other **cultures** did not treat

## Differences Between High- and Low-Context Cultures

me as an **equal**, as I was used to being treated in my own **culture**. In "low-**context**" **cultures**, where "anything goes" and "nothing matters," it is not as **offensive** when a woman steps out of traditional **roles**. This may not be true in a **culture** where everything matters. "High-**context**" **cultures expect** men and women to stay in their "**gender roles**."[117]

When speaking in *Bolivia* ("high-**context**") to a crowd of mostly men, I began by bringing greetings from my director, a *European* man whose reputation they knew well. This immediately put me in **context**. When they realized my boss was a well-respected man, they **accepted** me as a woman speaker. The crowd did not see me as a single woman traveling the world alone. That image would have created unnecessary **barriers**[118] to my teaching.

I travel alone quite a bit in my work. When I travel in the areas of the world where women are **expected** to **submit**[119] to men, I work hard at letting others see my

---
117. defined **roles**; responsibility or jobs that only a man or woman would do
118. a problem that blocks something from happening or from **accepting** a person
119. to **accept** the control of someone in authority

strong connections to my family and, therefore, to male leadership.

In the *United States*, the "higher-**context**" towns have been influenced by the cities through the news media and through travel, and so *American* towns are now more "low-**context**" than they were in the 1950s. My *American* grandmother's **role**, however, was clear in relation to her husband and other men. She loved being in the home and finding her **identity** in her **role** as a much-depended-upon wife and mother. The "power distance" between her husband and herself meant that his orders were obeyed willingly. The **role** of women in her town has gone more "low-**context**" now, and the traditional **role** of the wife has changed to most women working outside of the home. This has lowered the "power distance."

The **role** of women in "high-**context**" societies can be confusing to "low-**context**" people. The separation of **roles** in many "high-**context**" societies can be seen by "low-**context**" people as a statement of the **value** of the person. The woman seems to have less **value** because she has the **role** of being in the home, for instance. However, in traveling to countries

## Differences Between High- and Low-Context Cultures

where there is great "power distance" between men and women, I find I am more effective in my work if I respect the local thoughts of me as a woman and work within them.

For instance, in a place where women are not usually in charge, I don't demand to be in charge—even if I am the leader of a team. For example, I will give money in secret a nineteen-year-old male to pay the bill at a restaurant, just so I wouldn't **shame** him by paying for his meal in front of others. I have also taken a male team member with me sometimes when dealing with a local official. And I let the man with me do some of the talking. In this way, the male official does not need to be in the difficult situation of dealing with a woman directly.

This sounds like a terrible way of doing things to my **colleagues** of the more "low-**context**" **cultures**. I have found, however, that I need to know what my purpose is in the country I am visiting. It is not to argue about their view of women, but to seek the best way to work well together with them.

If we, as women, know who we are, we can honor the traditions of a **culture** in what they believe about their **gender**

*Foreign to Familiar*

**roles**. Their rules are important to them, and I must not force my own ideas upon them, no matter how important those ideas are to me.

## THE IMPORTANCE OF GREETINGS

It would be impossible to say too much about how important greeting people is in "high-**context**" **cultures**. Because everything matters in **formal cultures**, greetings are the **first impression**[120] the people get of you. With a **proper** greeting, you will be more **accepted**. If you fail with the greeting, you have failed the **first impression**. This is not a matter of doing things exactly as they do, but of honoring the other person by greeting them warmly in an **acceptable** way.

A *Dutch* person does not want to be hugged, for example. He wants you to say your name in a good strong voice, and he **expects** to receive a firm (never **limp**[121]) handshake.

The *Swiss* want a kiss *to* each side of the cheeks (never *on* the cheeks). This kissing may sound more

---
120. your first though about a person. (It can be hard to change that thought.)
121. weak; not strong

## Differences Between High- and Low-Context Cultures

personal, but it can actually be more **formal** than a strong handshake.

An *Arab* male greets another male with a loud and excited **display of affection**,[122] with lots of charming words to go with it. The traditional *Korean* smiles, stands at a respectful distance and bends at the waist (a little, if **familiar**[123] with the person or similar in importance or age, and lower, to show more respect due to age or importance in life).

One mistake a "low-**context**" person often makes is not recognizing how important it is to greet a person **properly**—even if the type of greeting is **foreign** to him or her. Teenagers often make this mistake. At this age, teenagers often feel uncomfortable socially, so they tend to not speak their names clearly or loudly, not look the other person in the eye or not greet someone at all. They might just walk into a room and walk right past the **host**. When taking teenagers on **cross-cultural** outings, it's helpful to talk about and even practice **proper** greetings. Remember, everything matters.

---

122. showing your feelings by hugging, kissing, back slapping
123. well known

*Foreign to Familiar*

"Low-**context**" people often have not been taught about local rules and **expectations**, and they may struggle with **cultural** greetings. Going **cross-cultural**, to them, does not seem to be a big deal, but it clearly *is* a big deal.

Most "high-**context**" **cultures** are understanding. If a **foreigner's** greeting is not the same as theirs, they can overlook it—as long as the greeting shows respect. For fast-moving *Americans* or *Australians*, it may mean slowing down and giving the **proper** time and attention to the **proper** rules of greeting.

Geert Hofstede's research has shown that "High Power Distant" and "Low Power Distant" **cultures** are not the same as the High- and Low-**Context cultures**. His book[124] gives an excellent list, country by country, of how these relate to one another.

As society is rapidly changing, all over the world, "high-**context**"**cultures** are becoming less so. Younger generations are throwing off some of the rules that their traditional **cultures** once held as non-negotiable.

---

124. *Cultures and Organizations, Software for the Mind*, with Gert Jan Hofstede and Michael Mindov, New York, NY, McGraw Hill: 2005

## POINTS TO REMEMBER

**High-Context Societies (everything matters):**
- Who you are related to matters.
- Who you know matters.
- It is better to dress more **formal** than to dress **casual**.
- Watch to see how others act in a situation, to know the **proper** behavior.
- Remember to honor the people you are dealing with; being too **casual** is **rude**.
- Ask a **local** person who has lived **overseas** for a while what is important to know.
- Use manners.
- Respect the rules.
- Give attention to **proper** greetings.

**Low-Context Societies (nothing matters; anything goes—but still use common sense).**
- Who you know matters, but not as much. What you know is more important.

- Do not be **offended** by the **casual** atmosphere.
- The **lack** of rules does not mean **rejection** and is not dishonoring.
- The people there do not know what your rules are, so leave your rules at home.
- **Address** people by their **given names** (unless others use their **titles**).

## *I'd Like to Go to Africa Today*

*I thought I would like*
*To go to Africa.*
*Yes, I will go to Kenya*
*And see if time*
*Has stood still*
*Where at least*
*The walk*
*Is on the ground*
*And all comes*
*To a sudden halt*
*At dusk*
*And sounds*
*Come from the voice*
*And travel a mile or two*
*And strength comes from*
*The family*
*Near to you.*
*Yes, today I thought*
*I'd like to go to Africa.*
        by Sallie Lanier, May 5, 1995

# Chapter 8

# Different Concepts of Time and Planning

The "cold-climate" structure (being organized) and the "hot-climate" **flexibility** (**lack** of organization) also affect the ways we get things done. The "cold-climate" societies have a goal of being able to produce a desired result, getting a job done and planning the job in advance. "Hot-climate" people have a tendency, instead, to respond to what life brings, rather than trying to plan life.

I am a *Southerner* who grew up and worked most of my life in "cold-climate" **cultures**—*Holland* and the *Middle East*. My personality is more "hot-climate," being open-ended, **spontaneous** and **easygoing**.[125] However, twelve years of

---
125. not worried or rushed; not easily upset; relaxed; calm

## Different Concepts of Time and Planning

working in *Holland* taught me to manage my time. I learned to get to the train on time because it was not going to wait for me, and to plan my day, my week and even my year.

I was **invited** to live in *Chile*, to work as a **consultant**[126] and trainer to some staff and leaders of a **nonprofit organization**.[127] I had already decided I wanted to live for a while in the *Southern* part of the world, to learn another language and **culture**, and this was my opportunity.

First, however, I would have to clear my calendar because I had many appointments made a year in advance, and some of my commitments could not be changed. It took me a year, but I finally had the opportunity to go.

I had been communicating with a person from *Chile* a few times during that year. When I arrived, the leaders who had **invited** me a year earlier were very happy, but surprised, to see me. "Sarah," one of them said to me, "how good to see you! What brings you back here? How long will you be with us?"

"A year," I answered.

---
126. a person who gives professional advice
127. an organization whose goal is to provide a service rather than make money

*Foreign to Familiar*

"A year? That's wonderful. What will you be doing here for a whole year?"

I was very surprised by this response. I had quit my job in *Holland*, rented out my apartment and completed all my duties for the next year. I was very surprised to learn that I was not **expected**.

When I talked to the leader about that, he said, "Sarah, I do remember **inviting** you, but that was a year ago. We've moved on. I **apologize** that only one person responded to your messages because that person has been traveling a lot, and the two of us have not communicated well."

Wow! I had a choice to make. I could turn around and go back to *Europe*, or I could stay on with no defined **role**.

That was my first **cultural** lesson. In *Europe*, we plan a year ahead of time, and only a major emergency would cause us to change those plans. If there was a change, we would communicate the changed plans to others.

In "hot-climate" **cultures** outside the *United States*, there is more of a **spontaneous** approach to life, and people do not like to plan a full year in advance. After all, circumstances might change.

### Different Concepts of Time and Planning

Because I had a desire to quickly learn the language, the first morning I was there I went into the main kitchen. That should be a good place to begin learning Spanish, I thought. I helped the ladies peel potatoes and, as I did, I asked them the names of different objects and then repeated them over and over, memorizing them. By the end of the day, I was easily speaking several phrases. I was proud of myself … until I learned that I had spent the whole day learning **Portuguese**.[128] The kitchen workers were from *Brazil*.

In the end, I decided that even if I did nothing more than sit around and drink coffee for a year, I was not leaving. I would see what purpose I could find. For the next nine months, I often sat around drinking coffee. But it was during those nine months that my friend Ricardo Rodriguez spent hour after hour talking to me about how the **Latin** mind works and how *Latin* leaders make decisions. Being a lawyer, he like to think and study deeply. He was brilliant in his **observations** of the *Western* influence in *South America,* as well as in other parts of the world. During this time, I also learned a good conversational level of *Spanish*.

---
128. the language of Portugal and Brazil

*Foreign to Familiar*

Looking back, I suppose that I could have reached my goals of learning about **culture** and getting a new language in the planned, structured way of going to a university and paying US $10,000, attending classes and taking exams. But I surely would not have learned the language or **culture** as well as I did by drinking coffee with friends. By being with the people, experiencing life as they lived it, I came away with an understanding, both in the heart and in the head.

I had almost thrown away this opportunity when things had not turned out as I planned. These plans, if made too important, could have cost me the richest learning experience of my life—the **spontaneous**, unplanned lifestyle of *Chile*.

All "hot-climate" **cultures** recognize that some areas of life require organization. The military is one example. It is no good to wait until the enemy is coming over the hill to organize how to **defend** yourself.

In the same way, **structure** (being organized) and planning help **avoid crises**[129] and may result in being more **efficient**,

---
129. trouble or danger

## Different Concepts of Time and Planning

saving money and effort over time. When **spontaneous cultures** become too **easygoing** and only react to life, they may miss great opportunities. This creates tension between **cultures**, but each one can learn from the other.

## Different Concepts of Time

One of the more common **cultural** differences people talk about is the **concept** of time. *German* **punctuality**[130] is **compared**[131] to the *Mexican mañana* (it can be done tomorrow). The "hot-climate" **culture** people are viewed by the "cold-climate" people as always being late. The "cold-climate" people are viewed by those from the "hot-climate" **cultures** as being slaves to time.

In a time-**oriented culture**, events are well organized, and time is an important element in that organization. The belief is that society runs more smoothly with a sense of order, and time provides the order. Therefore, events always have beginning times and usually even ending times. This

---
130. being on time
131. to see how two things are similar or different

*Foreign to Familiar*

is true of major events like weddings, conferences, worship services and music concerts. It is also true of smaller events, such as meeting a friend for coffee or picking someone up to go shopping.

Order is provided by a time being set for when the event will happen. The people involved are committed to being there and ready to go at that exact time. This can put people under pressure and make the time clock extremely powerful. The pressure is increased when circumstances happen that keep the person from getting to his destination on time. If he is late, he must always **apologize**. This **apology** represents respect for the other person. Their time was wasted waiting on you.

Time represents how much a person can "get done" in a day. Remember, "cold-climate" **cultures** are task oriented, and time provides a means to get their task done.

Let's talk about a wedding event. The location is *Jamaica, Zimbabwe, Colombia* or the *Philippines* ("hot-climate" **cultures**). The wedding is to begin at 2:00 pm. At 1:45 pm, four people from *Norway* and two people from *Canada* ("cold-climate" **cultures**) show up to get seats before the wedding starts. They find the church locked and no

## Different Concepts of Time and Planning

one around, **except** for some children playing out back. "Excuse me, kids, is this where the wedding is taking place?" they ask.

"Oh, yes. There is a wedding today," they are told.

A bit worried about whether or not there really will be a wedding that day, the guests wait on the steps.

At 1:55, a group of women arrives with flowers. They unlock the church and begin decorating. A choir leader comes a few minutes later and starts getting out some choir robes.

By 2:30, a few people arrive, and they stand around talking outside.

The "cold-climate" guests have found seats by now and keep looking at their watches, upset because the wedding is getting started late, and no one seems to care. What they don't know is that at around two o'clock the bride started getting ready, the preacher started a meal with the groom's parents, and a young man started his five-kilometer walk to the church.

Stopped along the way by an old man, the young man took as long as the old man wanted to talk. It would not have been honoring for him to tell the older man that he needed to hurry and could not talk.

*Foreign to Familiar*

Little by little, the crowd arrives at the church. The choir is practicing, and those who are choir members join the practice one-by-one as they arrive.

Soon, the choir begins to sing, and things begin to come to life. Around 3:45 pm, the bride and groom finally arrive, and the ceremony begins. By six o'clock, the wedding feast is happening.

This "hot-climate" wedding was an event, and the event began at 2:00 pm. That was when people stopped what they were doing and began wedding activities—getting the church decorated, entertaining the groom's family, and washing the children to get them dressed up for the occasion. The event had begun.

The "cold-climate" guests were angry. They **expected** the bride to start down the aisle at 2:00 pm. Before 2:00 pm, according to their thinking, everyone should have been in their places at the church and ready to start the wedding. To the "hot-climate" people, the wedding *did* begin at 2:00 pm. The event began with all the activity that surrounded it. The ceremony was only a small part of that event. It is not surprising that these differences in attitude about time cause so many problems.

## Different Concepts of Time and Planning

Once I attended an international conference where we were staying in the same building as the classes. To my surprise, the *Africans* ("hot-climate" **culture**) were the first to arrive in the **lecture** hall. When a *Swiss* person said, "I thought *African* time meant always being late," the *Africans* answered, "No, we are event-oriented. We know that the event will start now, and we have come for the event. We don't want to miss any of it."

After living in *Chile* ("hot-climate") for almost a year, I finally realized that I needed to arrive about forty-five minutes later than I said I would, at a café in town, to meet a friend. When I did that, we arrived almost at the same time. This was after regular afternoons of me getting upset because I had to stand on the street waiting for almost an hour every time we met.

You may wonder how I guessed at the correct time to arrive on this day. I learned to think like my friend thought. We always said we would meet at 2:00 pm, and her home was about thirty-five minutes away by bus and metro. I gave her ten minutes to notice that it was already 2:00 pm, time to stop whatever she was doing and go to the next event—meeting

*Foreign to Familiar*

me. She had to get on her coat and walk out the door. She was always on time for the event, but the event began at 2:00, when she started moving toward her appointment.

In different countries, time is measured out differently. It's always a good idea to **observe** first and see how it works where you are at the moment. In the "cold-climate" **cultures**, people enjoy using their time well. This allows them to get more done and to plan how much they can accomplish, both at work and in relaxation.

The order of the *German* ("cold-climate") **culture is reflected** in their trains running on time, the quick, well-ordered way business is handled, even the quick arrival of the coffee you order at a restaurant. To show respect to people is to respect their time. To keep a person waiting is to say, "You are not important, so your time is not important. I don't respect you or think you have anything more important to do than wait for me."

In some parts of each society, no matter the **culture**, time is highly **valued** as a sign of the ability to do something well, and of **integrity**[132] and respect. For example, the military
___
132. being honest and moral

### Different Concepts of Time and Planning

in any **culture** and high level of business, have their own **culture**, when it comes to time and organization. Their **survival** depends on it. "Time is money" is a saying in the *United States*.

Almost everywhere I go in the "hot-climate" world, the "cold-climate" people recognize the difference between *"Island* time," *"African* time," *"**Latin** time," "Southern* time" and *"**Western*** time." There is a belief that if you are ***Western***, you are time-**conscious**.[133] This is mostly true, **except** for the "hot-climate" ***Westerners***, like the ***Portuguese***, *Italians* and *American **Southerners***.

Being organized, planned and time-**conscious** go together. Being **spontaneous**, unplanned and event-**oriented** also go together. The social lives of the "cold-climate" **cultures** are planned. You are **invited**, or you even ask to come and visit, but it is always with advanced notice.

When living in *Europe* ("cold-climate"), I carried what is called a "Day-Timer ®." This is a notebook that helps you plan your day. There is a page for each day, and each page is divided into sections of 30 minutes. If any meeting came

---
133. aware, alert, mindful of

*Foreign to Familiar*

up, I would check my Day-Timer, and it would tell me if I was free at that time or not. My pages were usually filled up, and I moved from one scheduled appointment to the next.

When I lived in *Chile*, I had only one page for each month, but even those pages were mostly blank. Still, as I looked back, my days were full. They were filled with **spontaneous** events or routine events that didn't need a note in my Day-Timer as a reminder.

I was **spontaneously** asked to **lecture** at the University of Concepción in *Chile* and to fly to *Bolivia*, *Colombia* and *Argentina* to teach. I was **invited** into meetings and asked to help in areas of my skills. And I was also able to do some **consulting**. However, at the beginning of each month, I could not have told you what I would be doing that particular month. Life just happened, and I responded to it. That was the *South American* way.

## POINTS TO REMEMBER

"Hot-Climate" Cultures:
- Are not as **oriented** toward the clock as "cold-climate" **cultures**.
- Are event **oriented**.
- Are **spontaneous** and flexible in their approach to life.
- Respond to what life brings.
- Consider that saving time is not as important as experiencing the moment.
- Recognize that structure is required in some areas of life (the military, for example).
- Have informal visiting as part of an event.

"Cold-Climate" Cultures:
- Are time **oriented**.
- Are structured in their approach to life.
- Enjoy using time **efficiently**.
- Try to plan their day, and saving time is a **value**.
- **Expect** the event (dinner, the arrival of a guest or a meeting) to begin at the time announced. Visiting or informal chatting happens before or after the event.

### Chapter 9

# Practical Next Steps

The following suggestions may be helpful in making practical application of the **concepts** of this book:

1. In each new place, look for a "**culture** interpreter," a person who can explain the **culture** to you. A fellow **foreigner** who has already successfully **adjusted** to the **culture** is often a better coach than a **local**. A **local** person does not know which parts of his or her **culture** are different from your own. So, they don't know what is important to learn. A **foreigner** who has made a few mistakes will remember what is important. Later, a **local** person can possibly give you fuller understanding about the parts of life you find different or difficult to understand.

## Practical Next Steps

2. Before arriving at your **host culture**, read as much as possible on the history of the people. Become **familiar** with the **varieties** of **ethnic** groups within the area and how they relate to one another. To know that all *Arabs* are not Muslim or that *Lebanese* Christian *Arabs* often speak French in the home might be information you would want to know before arriving there. *Dutch* people in their seventies and older generally view *North Americans* as heroes because of their **role** in liberating Holland during World War II. The young people of the *Netherlands*, however, often see *North Americans* as **spoiled**[134] and **materialistic**[135] and cannot understand why *Americans* don't take better care of their **natural resources**.[136] A study of the history will help you understand the reasons for the way people think and act. Look for books and other resources in libraries or the Internet.

---

134. damaged by having been given everything they want
135. when money and things are most important to a person
136. forests, water, land; what is in nature

*Foreign to Familiar*

3. Once you are in the country of your destination, search out books or other resources that other **foreigners** have found helpful for that specific **culture**.

4. Before leaving home, try to find people from the country you plan to visit who can talk to you about their home. A positive view is important in **adjusting** to and **accepting** any new **culture**. **Native** people of that country usually will tell you the parts they love. Based on the previous chapters, ask questions about the **culture**, to see where there may be **exceptions** to these **principles** and which **principles** should be **emphasized**. Ask the people what the major **adjustments** were for them in coming to *your* country. That will give you an idea as to what will be the opposite **adjustment** for you in *their* country.

5. Try to discover the **values** of the society. Religion, for instance, is taken very seriously in some **cultures** and not in others. The movie, "Beyond Paradise," is a story of *Hawaiian* teenagers who finally **accept** a

## Practical Next Steps

white boy into their **inner circle**.[137] He was treated as one of them ... until one day at the beach he wanted to hop around on the ruins of an ancient holy site. When he kept doing it, even when his friends asked him over and over not to, they beat him up, and they also broke off their friendship with him. Why? Because he failed to understand how important their religious customs were to them.

6. Be aware of "**culture shock**" and "culture stress." The **familiar** routines of life serve to make things easier. We shop in the same grocery store because we know where things are. We don't realize just how much we depend on routine and **familiarity**. When we go to a place where everything is different and none of our routines are the same, we attempt to **adjust**. Often, we do it by **comparing** the new to the old **familiar** world back home. "This tastes like chicken," "I like that store because it sells

---
137. a small group of friends

*Foreign to Familiar*

*British*-style pudding or *Korean*-style rice." A *Kenyan* will taste *American* grits and say, "That is just like *ugali*." A *Mexican* in *India* will look at a *chapati*, hoping for something like a tortilla, and say, "Close enough." **Adjusting** daily with the **unfamiliar** means making new decisions all the time. These changes might relate to transportation or using a telephone. It all has to be relearned, and it all takes energy and leads to tiredness and even discouragement. This is **culture stress**, which lasts longer than **culture shock**. **Culture shock** is the negative impact the **unfamiliar** world makes on you.

7. When you return home, after you have **adjusted** to many of the **host-culture** routines and practices, it will take the same kind of energy to **reenter**[138] your home **culture**. This is called "**reverse culture shock**." Many are unprepared for the negative way

---
138. returning to your home country; to enter again

## Practical Next Steps

it will affect them ... until things become **familiar** again.

There are scores of books and articles written on the subject of **reentry**. I suggest you prepare for returning home with the same purposefulness as preparing for your venture into a new **culture**.

8. Once you return home, look for others who have traveled, or even better, for people from your **host culture**. **Debrief** with them. People from your home **culture** will not want to hear all your stories or even understand your need to share them. You are the one who left, and life continued at home. Over the years, I learned, as I visited my beloved grandparents in the *States*, that the way to be a part of their lives was to listen to their **local** news, entering *their* world. They were not able to identify with my **foreign** world, and I learned to **accept** that.

9. Learn some words in the **local** language. Leaning even a little is better than not learning at all. This

*Foreign to Familiar*

shows that you **value** the people you have come to work with. I asked some *Pacific Islanders* working in *Canada* what they wished they'd known before coming. They all said, "We wish we had learned English. It would have been so much easier to make connections. We could have built relationships with the people immediately. Once we were here, it took all of our energy just to **adjust**. We were too tired at the end of the day to learn the language."

10. Finally, spend time listening and **observing**. Don't judge others until you have discovered the reason behind their "strange" habits. **Assume** the best about them. **Assume** that they know what they are doing and their behavior is based on their experience and personal and **cultural** belief systems.

Once, on a trip through the Sinai desert, a young man asked our guide why the **Bedouin Arabs**[139] wore so many clothes. Considering how hot it was in the desert, this seemed foolish to him. The guide said,

---
139. Nomadic Arabs

## Practical Next Steps

"The robes allow air flow, which cools them. The sleeves cover their entire arms, keeping them from drying up too much because of moisture coming off the skin. The head piece is loose, allowing air to circulate around the neck, again cooling them. Their clothing is white, so it **reflects** the sun. Wisely, they sleep during the hottest part of the day. They've been here a few thousand years, so don't you think they would have come up with the best ways to **survive** in this desert?"

We often want to change our **host's culture** when we see them "doing it wrong." Remember what you have come for and stick to those goals ... until you have earned the right to be heard.

I was once in charge of cooking for a group of twenty people on a work project. A lady who spoke no English was helping me in the kitchen. I had bought many potato peelers when I noticed that people still used knives to peel potatoes. I saw how much of the potato was being wasted with the knives, so I thought I would improve things. As my translator tried to help

*Foreign to Familiar*

the lady understand my instructions on how to use the peeler, she finally said, "Sarah, can't you just let her peel the potatoes like she has for generations?" She was right. I put the peelers away.

## Chapter 10

# In Conclusion

With a little understanding, much conflict can be **avoided** between people of different **cultural** backgrounds. My hope is that, knowing there are some simple basic truths, you can now develop your knowledge of any new **culture**.

Not all of these characteristics I have mentioned are always present in all hot- and "cold-climate" **cultures**. One person even suggested that I use the term "hot-tribal people versus cold-urban people." Many tribes in the cold mountainous regions of the world behave like "hot-climate" people, while many city dwellers in the hot countries, like *Brazil* and *Argentina*, may act more like those from "cold-climate" areas.

Also, many individuals in every **culture** act very differently from the rest of their people because their personalities may fit the opposite types of **cultures**. The important

*Foreign to Familiar*

thing is to ask yourself, "What are my own **cultural** habits? And are they **acceptable** for the **culture** I am going into?"

We all think that our way of doing things is better than that of others. If we can get beyond that, we'll find we can begin to learn, respect and enjoy the differences. Soon, what seems **foreign** will become **familiar**. And we'll find that we have much in common with the **varied** people of the earth.

# Dictionary of Words and Phrases

**Accent:** a way of pronouncing words
**Accept, acceptable, acceptance, accepted:** to receive
**Accurate:** correct in all details; exact
**Address, addressing:** how you greet someone
**Adjust, adjusted, adjusting, adjustment:** to change, changes
**Adults-Only:** any activity to which children are not invited
**Agricultural:** farming; raising crops/animals
**Apologize, apology:** to say "I'm sorry"
**Appreciate, appreciated:** to be very important to a person; valued
**Arab:** people primarily from Arabia and other countries of the Middle East
**Asserting themselves:** putting themselves in charge; taking control of a situation
**Assume, assumed:** to believe something without proof
**Avoid, avoided:** to keep away from
**Barrier:** a problem that blocks something from happening or from accepting a person
**Bedouin Arabs:** nomadic Arabs
**Bother, bothering:** annoying; disturbing
**Camp David Accords:** an agreement between Israel and Egypt in 1978 that led to a peace treaty
**Casual, casually:** comfortable and relaxed
**Colleague:** a person who works with you; a fellow worker
**Comfort, comfortable:** the feeling of being relaxed and happy
**Compare, comparing:** to see how two things are similar or different
**Concept:** an idea
**Conscious:** aware, alert, mindful of
**Consultant, consulting:** a person who gives professional advice
**Context:** the setting or surroundings

**Contrast:** differences can be seen)
**Convenience:** is easy and not much work
**Crisis/es:** trouble or danger
**Cross-cultural, cross-culturally:** comparing or dealing with two or more cultures
**Cultural identity:** who you are; the way you think about yourself
**Culture:** the the values and behaviors of a group of people
**Culture bridge:** a person who can help others understand new cultures
**Culture shock:** the impact of getting use to a different culture
**Curt, curtness:** replying with a very short answer, almost rude
**Defend:** be able to explain your reason for doing or believing something
**Discuss, discussion:** talk about something; share ideas
**Display of affection:** showing your feelings by hugging, kissing, back slapping
**Distraction:** something that takes your attention away
**Divided:** split into parts; separated
**Dorm:** a place students live at a school
**Drop in, dropping in:** to visit someone unannounced and unexpected
**Dutch:** the people of the Netherlands
**Easygoing:** not worried or rushed; not easily upset; relaxed; calm
**Efficient, efficiency, efficiently:** doing things well
**Elder:** a person who is older
**Emphasize:** give special importance
**Equal:** having the same social status; no one is superior to the others
**Ethnic:** people grouped by race, nationality, culture or religion
**Except/exception:** something that does not follow the rule or is not included
**Expect, expected, expecting, expectations:** being sure it will happen; anticipated
**Familiar, familiarity:** well known
**Filipino:** people from the Philippines
**First impression:** your first thought about a person. (It can be hard to change that thought.)
**First-name basis:** using your given name in an informal friendly way

Focus: the center of interest or attention
Foreign, foreigner: from another country; unknown; new
Formal: the opposite of casual; very polite and official, involving special customs and clothing
Founding: what something was built on
Frustrated, frustrating: upset; irritated; annoyed
Gathering: when people meet together
Gender roles: defined roles; responsibility or jobs that only a man or woman would do)
Generalization: a statement of what people tend to do; a tendency; most of the people most of the time
Generosity: being kind and giving
Given name: first name; the name given to you at birth; the name people call you
Great Depression: (1929-1939) A time of worldwide financial crisis which started in the USA
Guilty: doing something wrong
Hospitality: showing kindness to guests)
Host/hostess: people who entertain guests (host, a man and hostess, a woman)
Ignore/ignored: to intentionally not give any attention to someone
Inclusive: everyone is welcomed and included
Inconvenience: something that is uncomfortable and difficult
Indigenous: the native people of a country
Industrial Revolution: (1760-1840) A time when Europe and the USA developed factories
Inner circle: a small group of friends
Innocent: not meant to cause harm
Insist, insisting: to demand; not allow someone to say no
Integrity: being honest and moral
Interracial: people from different races or ethnic group coming together
Interrupting, interrupting, interrupted: to stop the activity
Intrusion: an uninvited visit or entrance

# Invite-Overseas

**Invite, invited, inviting, invitation:** when you are asked to go somewhere or do something
**Jewish, Jew:** people originally from Israel)
**Justice:** concern for fairness; equality and respect for all people
**Lack:** not enough
**Laid-back:** relaxed and calm
**Latin, Latino, Latin American:** people from Latin America; the Caribbean; South America; Central America
**Lecture, lecturer:** an educational talk to students
**Limp:** weak; not strong
**Literal:** exactly as it is written
**Local:** a person from that location; a native-born person
**Lonely, loneliness:** feeling alone, not included in the group
**Majority:** the greater number
**Materialistic:** when money and things are most important to a person
**Mediator:** a person that helps others come to an agreement
**Monocultural:** one single culture
**Multicultural:** several distinct cultures
**Native:** a person born in that place
**Natural resources:** forests, water, land; what is in nature
**Nonprofit organization:** an organization whose goal is to provide a service rather than make money
**Northern European:** people from Germany, the Netherlands, Switzerland and Scandinavia
**Nourish, nourishment:** to give what is needed for health
**Objective:** an opinion outside of yourself; removed from your feelings
**Objective logic:** a decision based on reasoning, not feeling
**Observe, observed, observation, observing:** to learn by watching carefully
**Offend, offensive:** causing someone to feel deeply hurt, upset or angry
**Offer, offering:** to give something that can be accepted or rejected
**Opinion:** belief; judgment; viewpoint
**Optional:** can choose to do it but you don't have to
**Outsider:** a person who is not a part of the group
**Overseas:** in a foreign country, especially one across a sea

Overwhelming: very great amount; more than someone can handle
Perspective: personal viewpoint
Podium: the place the speaker stands so all in the audience can see and hear him
Portuguese: the language of Portugal and Brazil
Possessions: what you own, what belongs to you)
Prefer, preference: what a person likes
Presence: where you are right now
Principle: rule, idea
Priority: the most important part
Proper, properly: right; correct; accepted
Punctuality: being on time
Quality: how good something is
Reenter, reentry: returning to your home country; to enter again
Reflect: to represent the whole group, to speak for the group
Refuse: to say no; not take it
Reject/rejection: not being accepted; you do not like
Ridiculous: absurd; silly; foolish; unbelievable
Role: part played by a person
Round-about way: indirect, not clear
Rude, rudeness: disrespectful; not polite
Sacrifice: giving up something that is very important to you
Shame, shamed, shameful: public humiliation; embarrassing; making someone look bad in public
Signal: an action or sound that is used to communicate information or instructions
Southern, Southerners, the South: people from the Southeast in USA
Southern accent: a way of pronouncing words
Spoiled: damaged by having been given everything they want
Spontaneous, spontaneously: unplanned
Steward: owner, manager
Subjective: an opinion influenced by personal feelings or tastes
Submit: to accept the control of someone in authority
Superficial: fake; on the surface

Survive-With open arms

**Survive, survival:** being able to continue to live even when it is very difficult

**Swiss:** people from Switzerland

**Take initiative, taking initiative:** to speak up, make suggestions or step forward

**Task-oriented:** the focus, focused on a goal

**Thai:** a person from Thailand

**Theory:** possible reasons for ideas

**Title:** a name that tells a person's position; doctor, teacher, Mr., Mrs.

**To-the-point:** said without wasting words or time

**Trend:** to do what others are doing; a fad

**Trek:** a long difficult hike, often many days or weeks

**Unexpected/unexpectedly:** you did not know it would happen

**Unstructured:** doesn't follow a schedule

**Value, valued:** the worth, importance, or usefulness of something; principles considered most important

**Varied, variety, various:** different or diverse people

**Western, Westerners, Western Word:** people from the West part of the world; Western Europe, North America

**Westernized:** to become like the people who live in the Western World

**With open arms:** eagerly, warmly, wanting to please; happily

# AUTHOR CONTACT PAGE

Correspondence with the author may be directed to:

**Sarah A. Lanier**
**PO Box 874**
**Clarkesville, GA 30523**
**USA**

**sarah_a_lanier@yahoo.com**

For editions in the following languages, please contact the author at Sarah_a_lanier@yahoo.com

Arabic
French
Korean
Portuguese
Russian
Spanish

For Dutch: info@uitgeverijethnos.nl
For German: www.francke-buch.de
For Norwegian: www.proklamedia.no
For Russian distribution in Europe: janeofasrk@gmail.com